Seeing Through
Spiritual Eyes
A Memoir of
Intuitive Awakening

Tom Jacobs

By Tom Jacobs

Books

The Soul's Journey I: Astrology, Reincarnation, and Karma with a Medium and Channel
The Soul's Journey II: Emotional Archaeology
The Soul's Journey III: A Case Study
Living Myth: Exploring Archetypal Journeys
Saturn Returns: Thinking Astrologically
Chiron, 2012, and the Aquarian Age: The Key and How to Use It
Lilith: Healing the Wild
Pluto's 2012 Retrograde and the First Square to Uranus in Aries (e-book)

Channeled Material

Approaching Love
Understanding Loss and Death
Goddess Past, Present, and Future
Conscious Revolution: Tools for 2012 and Beyond
Djehuty Speaks (a compilation of the above 4 books)
Healing Suicide (ebook)
Conscious Living, Conscious Dying

ISBN 1451509030
EAN13 9781451509038

Contents

Acknowledgements

For support, encouragement, and holding space for my evolving vision of me many warm thanks go to Jonathan and Charity Babcock-Jedeikin, Joanne Brohmer, Jeff Kihn, Monica Way, Alex Castrogiovanni, and my mother, Joy Thomas. I'm grateful to Stuart Geltner and Robin Clark for being fantastic role models as compassionate counselors, reflectors, and teachers. For suggesting that I try mediumship and offering me opportunities to learn and do it, I'd like to thank Amy Beauchamp. Early in my process she saw clearly the use in this kind of book and was the first to encourage me to write down my experiences and observations.

I'm grateful also to Thoth, et al. for shining light on things and welcoming me into the club, and to my guides for helping me prove some old-time versions of me wrong at every turn.

Thanks also go to my grandfather, Robert Johnson Jacobs, who has revealed himself to be one of my biggest fans in all the worlds. His commitment to make sure I never forget that I'm loved has helped to change everything.

Introduction

As I told friends and colleagues about my experiences learning to do intuitive and psychic work, many encouraged me to write them down. They believed that what I was learning about myself, the spiritual side of things, and life itself would offer cues and support for people on a journey of opening to the spiritual side of life.

They helped reflect to me that before going down this path, I was as far from it as I could have been. I was the person in any given room who was not interested in hearing about the unseen parts of life. If you wanted the most rational take on a subject, I was your guy. I insisted on relying on what could be seen, touched, and proven.

My intuition had always been strong but I often didn't listen to it. In fact, I spent a great deal of energy *not* listening to it! It seemed I had little reason to. There were times when something from someone's inner world came through to me. Sometimes I used the information to good effect, but I didn't want to know what was going on in other realms. I now know that I had karma (I define this as conditioned beliefs – what we think our experiences mean – carried over from past lives) surrounding religion, belief, and spirituality, and I was determined not to repeat what seemed like past, related mistakes. My response was to try to shut out all of religion and spirituality together. I think there's a baby-bathtub proverb I could have benefitted from remembering!

In many ways, this book is a story of me processing and reacting to the challenges of my first Saturn return. For those not familiar with this astrological term, it refers to the end of a person's first chapter with living the energy of maturity, responsibility, structure, and discipline, and the beginning of the second. At around age 29 ½ (the duration of Saturn's orbit around the Sun) each of us is challenged to confront how we understand and live the energies associated with Saturn.

Saturn in my astrological birth chart is in the sign of Gemini and in the 9th house. Gemini is the sign of curiosity and exploration. The 9th house relates to the parts of life having to do with what we believe and how we go about seeking what is true. As Saturn can put the brakes on whatever area of life it touches, my self-confrontations during my Saturn return were all about opening my mind and being open to new ideas about what is and might be true. It is not uncommon for people to deal for years with the challenges that arise during their first Saturn returns. Essentially, at this time we have to give up our old ideas of maturity and discipline in order to grow into new ones. It can be a difficult process and especially so for those who are not inclined to give attitudes and beliefs up easily – as I was until a few years into the process.

This book is written in the hope that my experiences and what I learned from them might shed some light on some unseen realities for those who might not have experienced them. Also it is for those who are for any reason interested or who have experienced them but didn't know where to file the experiences or what to do with them. When I look back, I realize that my experiences have given me a grounding into and understanding of how humans fit into the greater scheme of things in the Universe. This has resulted in a sense of hope about life and what we're doing here that I probably always wanted to have but couldn't for a long time see how to obtain. Others in my life have been amazed at the transformation I've been through over the last seven years as of this writing. I wonder if a kind of road map of my journey to get here can serve to help others navigate their own path.

The book contains information on a few different aspects of spiritual work, primarily mediumship and channeling. Taken together, they represent my journey to date and the skills and understanding I gained as I learned to do these kinds of work. To learn these skills involved reorienting how I lived and I have observed that while true for many who end up doing this work, this is not widely understood that one's life must change if he or she is to do good intuitive and psychic work.

For anyone opening up to their intuitive or psychic skills, we can't know with certainty what the process and end result will look like. For this reason I include with my experiences the spiritual truths that underscored them. The truths about energy, consciousness, and spirituality included here form the basis for each and every journey involving developing one's spiritual side. For example, while you may or may not be (or have any interest in being) a psychic medium, the truths about life, death, and how humans learn during and between lives can help you understand the life process that we all undertake. In other words, this information is useful in avenues of spiritual work beyond mediumship.

The steps to reconnect with one's spiritual side and to come to trust it will be different for each person. This book is intended to share the path on which I found myself in hopes that the stories can shed light on different ways such connection and coming to trust the self can happen. If a person is called to tap into, develop, or come to trust the unseen forces in his or her life, he or she will be lead down the right path to get there and will need to trust that this is so. Additionally, the material here might help you identify reasons that parts of you might be hesitant or resistant to such life changes. There may be parts of you not willing to open to or trust spirit. These reasons could have held you back even if you have solid intentions to learn to open or trust. It is also true that many who feel the beginnings of a psychic or intuitive opening do not have a context for what is happening to them or a support structure to help them through it. I expect this book will find its way into the hands of some people in that situation and this is one reason I decided to write it. The unseen parts of life discussed in this book become real for those who are open to seeing themselves as more than physical machines with computer minds.

The book is organized not quite chronologically. The first chapter, *Opening*, refers to the process of becoming willing to change how I lived to let in more awareness of energy and the influence of spirit. It excerpts and summarizes a smorgasbord of experiences I had in the first few years of the process as I found my footing in spiritual realms. The next chapter, *Awakened Spirit*, shares experiences and teachings from the channeling class I took in Santa Monica. It was part of that opening yet seems to deserve its own chapter because of the amount of information included – specifically the spiritual truths I learned during that time and began incorporating into my life. As a result, some of the experiences recounted in the first chapter take place after those in the second.

My facility as a medium was developed next, followed by my skills as a channel, and chapters on those two areas follow in that order. *A Meditation*, the appendix, includes instructions and notes on a meditation I use and teach to develop healthy energetic boundaries. Originally taught to me by my channeling teacher Robin Clark, it can support any and all sorts of spiritual work.

Whatever stage of opening you might be in, I hope this book proves useful along the way.

1 Opening

I knew a woman at my college on vague terms. She was a few years younger than me and while we moved in some of the same circles, we didn't decide we had much in common. We became friends after I graduated and was living in Boston while she was dating a roommate of mine she knew from our college. We kept in touch after that, and I visited her in New York City when she moved there. In time she moved to Los Angeles and I visited her there, too – three years in a row. The first two of those years, neither of us was really sure why we were friends. We got along well and enjoyed seeing each other but didn't feel very close. On the third visit, I met her fiancé and things started to make sense.

It was clear to the fiancé and me from the get-go that he and I had a deep connection. I remember getting out of the car after the ride from the airport into Hollywood, not being sure how to act. I didn't know what to make of it. There was a strong energy in the air I hadn't encountered before. Over the following few days I adjusted to it, telling myself that he and I simply had a strong connection.

It felt right to be in Los Angeles – traffic, air quality, and all. By the middle of my visit, my friend's fiancé asked me matter-of-factly when I was moving to L.A., and it felt like the decision had already been made. I said I guessed it would be a couple of months, as it seemed a done deal.

I went back to Cambridge, MA and began wrapping up my life there. People asked me why I had decided to move and the best answer I had was that it was gut instinct. Making the decision to move to L.A. was freeing but I was the first to admit that I had no idea what I might be getting myself into. Part of me had always wanted to move to California though if you'd asked me I would have picked the San Francisco Bay area and not considered L.A. even for a moment. The imagery that came up when I thought of L.A. was less than pleasant: stress, superficiality, and being stuck in a car on a jam-packed highway. But the decision seemed already made, so I went with it.

I put in notice at my office in Cambridge, where I had been in the process of creating a career path for myself that I thought was pretty cool. On my return, however, I knew I was done with it. Something new had been sparked in me when I was in L.A., and everything I had been doing in Cambridge had begun to seem part of a chapter that was coming to an end.

My coworkers and bosses reflected to me how different I felt, with a couple of them telling me that my state of inspiration had an inspiring effect on them, as did a friend outside work. I told them that, in a nutshell, my reason for moving was that life is too short not to go with your gut instinct.

One of my bosses told me that after seeing me return in this new, inspired state and talking about gut instinct, he'd finally made a commitment to himself to go to half-time in his position in order to spend more time with his family. It had been on his mind (and theirs) for years, but the pressures of projects and deadlines at work kept him from doing it. He also decided to pick up his saxophone again after a number of years, recognizing how much happiness it brought him to play it. He seemed relieved to have made these decisions, and that was a great reflection to me of how I felt as I readied for a kind of new adventure.

To tell one of my closest friends in Cambridge about the move, I asked her to dinner. I told her of my plans and she was as surprised to hear it as I had been to think it. She then heard the story I'd been telling people. She could see that I was inspired and was happy for me. A few days later, she told me that hearing my story and seeing how lit up I'd become inspired her to do something about her fear of flying. A few years before this she had moved from Oakland, CA to Cambridge, and hadn't gone back to visit her close friends in California because of this fear. She felt trapped by it – sad that she hadn't gone back – but had felt there was no way she could do it. She finally felt empowered enough to do something about it after years of talking about it and not talking about it, thinking and not thinking about it – all in circles. A few months after I moved to L.A., she and a mutual friend of ours flew together to Oakland and I picked them up on the way to a long weekend in Mendocino and Ft. Bragg, CA, where my friend has family.

On the day I put in notice, a coworker came by my cubicle to ask me why I was leaving. I told her the bit about gut instinct and life being too short not to listen to it. She came to me the next day and asked me to talk in a conference room. It struck me as odd because we didn't know each other at all (I think our 87-second conversation the previous day was our first), but I agreed. Once there, she told me that after talking to me the day before, she went home and called her father to tell him all the things she had known for four years she wanted and needed to tell him. He responded better than she thought he might, and that conversation seemed to portend a turning point in their relationship. She acknowledged my bravery and thanked me for inspiring her.

She also told me that she'd been involved in a self-help program in the area, a branch of an organization with chapters all over the world. Much of what I'd decided on my own, she said, was included in their teachings. She invited me to a "bring a friend" night at the program center, which was that night – an appreciative gesture to expose me to their teachings in case I found them worth investigating. Her idea was that since I'd figured out so much of it on my own, I might find their ideas and structure interesting. I thanked her and agreed to go. That day I had a plan to go after work with a colleague who knew a lot about cars who offered to take me to some dealer lots for test drives. I was scoping out the automobile situation since I had decided I'd need to buy one when I got to L.A. and hadn't paid attention to anything about cars for the six years I was in Massachusetts (the bus and subway – the T – got me all the places I wanted to go). We ended up losing track of time looking at cars and talking to car people so when she dropped me off at the T station, I realized I had missed the rendezvous with the other woman from work to go to the meeting.

I didn't have the address or even any idea where the program center was, so I jogged the half mile to the office and looked up the group's website for the address. Then I figured out which T line went there and looked up the directions from the T station to the center. I jogged the half mile back to the T and got on a train to wherever it was. I remember now it was the Red Line and I needed to go south, and that's about it. All the time I was monitoring my watch, as I was already uncomfortable with being late. The train arrived and I jogged over to the address and went in.

"The session's already started," the women at the table in the hall whispered to me. I told them my friend's name and that I had missed our meet up time. One said that my friend had been really bummed that I wasn't able to make it and that she'd be thrilled to know I had after all. They looked really surprised (and at that point I did have a little perspiration showing after my jogs and the stress of hurrying), but I said I'd told her I'd come and so I did. I didn't know at that time that a major teaching on which their work is centered is integrity, and they teach the importance of following through on your word. I took a name tag and wrote my name on it, took some literature they handed me, and went in. Everyone else in the room had a partner, so among around one hundred seats there was one open, next to my new friend.

She was indeed happy I showed up, and also surprised. She figured I'd think it was too much trouble to get all the way down there (it was a 45-minute T ride and she knew that she hadn't told me the address), but I said I told her I'd be there and so I figured it out. The "bring a friend" night was built around a recruiting strategy, and she had told me that afternoon that they would try to get me to sign up for a course. Her motivation in inviting me was for informational purposes only and she wanted to be sure I didn't feel pressure to sign up for their classes. The literature I'd picked up at the greeters' table was sort of a little workbook to use during the evening. There were times during the presentation when guests were to work with their experienced partners on identifying life issues they could work on in the workshops and classes being pitched. She and I used that time instead for a series of questions from me and answers from her about their ideas and how their process works, and she was happy to answer my questions. She was as analytical about psychology and self-understanding as I was and by the time it was over, I felt I understood a lot about what they did and offered people, and I was happy I had agreed to go.

When it was officially over, my friend went to talk to some people she knew. I stood alone for a minute and then a representative from the program came over to ask me if I had any questions about their workshops and classes. I said I didn't and that I had enjoyed hearing about what they do. He then asked me if I could see myself taking their programs and what in my personal life I saw that I could use their teachings to change for the better. I said I wouldn't take classes there. He wanted to know why and so I told him I felt that the way they used some terms in their teaching were misleading and would generate confusion and miscommunication in students' lives when outside the center's workshops. I said that they were in effect teaching their students to change what certain words meant, leaving them to go out into a world and back to families, friends, and colleagues who had zero idea what they were talking about. I said that was not something I would choose to be involved in. I explained that and each of my other objections in detail when asked over the following few minutes. He did the best he could to open me up to allow him to sell me on the course by repeatedly asking me about personal issues I would work on if I were to take it. I stuck with my pleasant demeanor and firm "no, thank you" agenda. After about twenty minutes, a more senior representative saw that the man was having difficulty and came over first to listen, and then to take over.

I began the same explanations again when this new man, more experienced and more practiced in talking with prospective students, asked me the same questions. *Was I interested in taking the course? Oh, really, no? Why not?* I repeated myself and talked with him for probably another 15 minutes. All I was saying was that, in my opinion, the course was not for me. And as I repeatedly explained why, they kept asking me why! I felt disinclined to go into painstaking detail about how important I feel language is to the way we live and how it affects and shape consciousness. I believe they thought they could talk anyone into the course, and I wasn't turning out to play along as they seemed to have expected. Their frustration was a response to my unshakable energetic stance, I feel. It seemed they were not used to dealing with people who had the groundedness to resist the pitch for the course (and then of course the hard sell when the regular one didn't work) if they didn't want to take it. The second guy represented the hard-sell energy, but I wasn't available to concede my feeling that what their courses offered was not for me. The entire time I was calm, gracious, and respectful to these two men. I had nothing to say other than that I enjoyed the evening but the course was not for me and thank you for the information. By the time the second guy was very frustrated and close to fed up with me, there was a little crowd of people involved in the center gathered around us. It was around a half hour after the session ended, as it turned out, and they were ready to close down the building for the night. I realized I was the only guest still there.

The woman who lead the evening's activities then stepped in and took over for the second guy, the now fed-up one with the hard-sell strategy. I remained calm and respectful as she engaged me and wanted to hear what I had been talking about with the two men. I gave her a summary and she was aggressive and trying to pull all sorts of sneaky energetic gambits to undermine my confidence. I was kind and generous to the two guys, who were not all that aggressive and not at all obnoxious, but also to this woman who *was* aggressive and obnoxious.

Energetically, she was in my face and challenging me abrasively on each and every one of my points. She became visibly frustrated and after about 15 minutes ended the conversation with a curt and disrespectful comment and stormed off. My friend was there at that point, as the dozen or so people left in the room had been standing to the side and listening. I felt like a stone tower, unmovable and unshakable. I had never experienced a feeling like that before, and I knew without doubt that it had a lot to do with my choice to remain respectful and loving toward these people even as the course of the three conversations described an arc of escalating tension that was at the end directed toward me as aggression. Aggression and argumentativeness have always been difficult for me to be around. During my life to that point I would shut down emotionally and energetically when around anger. I learned in those 45 or so minutes what happens when you choose to show love in the face of aggression, and for that reason it was a seminal night in my life.

As my friend and I left for the T station, I realized I'd just made a sort of spectacle in front of the people she with whom she attended classes and from whom she took them. I apologized in case I had made going back there difficult for her, but she was practically speechless after what she'd just seen. She complimented me on keeping my attitude open and responding to the leader without any of the aggression being thrown at me. She said she was impressed that I stood my ground and didn't let them bully me. She said that they weren't used to people who don't respond to bullying. She hadn't seen anyone come out of a conversation with people there without having either given in and signed up or felt bullied and signed up. I told her I felt like a stone tower and how aggression was something I had not previously responded to in a healthy way. She was doubly impressed! In retrospect, the evening was a harbinger of what was to come with my move to L.A. in terms of the strength I would need to cultivate to stand my ground and not budge in the face of aggressive energy, as the city of L.A. turned out in some ways to be a less than nurturing place for me.[1]

I took these reactions to my decision to move as reflective of the inspired part of me that was beginning to come out. That version of me had been nearly always buried under a need to control everything and a judging, negative voice that had a

---

[1] Curiously to me, L.A. was full of people who were taking the classes offered by these people. At one point in my first year there I realized that of the seven people I felt closest to in the city, all but one were graduates of the group's programs. I saw that I was surrounded by the vocabulary and meaning issues that kept me from being open to taking in their teachings. Some of my friends insisted that someday I would, and there was little else at that time that would tick me off more than telling me I'd eventually go pay people to make me change what words meant!

comment on just about everything around me. When I left Cambridge I was sad to leave a city I loved so much but excited about new possibilities.

The drive across the country was difficult for two reasons. The brainy parts of me felt so at home in Cambridge that they couldn't imagine a better way of living. In my eyes it was a cornucopia of artistic (both as performance and consumption) and intellectual opportunities. And there I was on the way to L.A., a gigantic, sprawling, filthy city with a dearth of independent book stores – *what was so great about that?*, part of me fumed. There was also a woman in Boston for whom I had feelings, but I had not told her of them. There were feelings of loss written all over that move even as I was excited to find out what would unfold in L.A.

Landing in LA

The apartment next door to my college friend and her fiancé happened to be vacant when I arrived in Los Angeles, and I moved in. Over the following few months I became very close to them and had many reasons to be grateful for this solid support structure in my new city. They became more like family than friends.

Following my arrival I had culture shock from a combination of spending time in a car once again, the general fact of all the traffic and people, the weather, and the large geographic area covered by the metropolitan L.A. area. Wherever you wanted to go, it seemed to take two eternities. This was also the summer of particularly bad wild fires in the area (2003) and for weeks in my apartment I could hear the wailing sirens of fire trucks on their way to Malibu and Simi Valley. At that time there was also a notable number of gunshots at night in that neighborhood – one or two each week – and I was anything but used to that.

Once I'd been in Los Angeles for a few months, I began having experiences that made me uncomfortable. At times I felt like I was in some sort of consciousness-altering experiment involving powerful drugs, one in which I'd somehow gotten involved without giving my consent. I know now that my intuitive and psychic sides were being stirred and opened up, but at the time I had neither a frame of reference nor a vocabulary for strange happenings resulting in altered consciousness other than to say that I felt drugged.

The first strange experiences came as I drove in the new automobile I purchased upon arriving. This could be because of the fact that very often when in motion, I find myself able to relax. Bicycle and motorcycle riding are tools I use to clear my head, as is at times walking, though I usually need to be a bit faster than that to really clear my head out. In the car in L.A., I would feel my awareness skip like a scratched record and, most often, when on the highway. I was already a little squeamish driving in L.A., famous for its highways and the apparent culture of aggression mixed with indifference that seemed to surround and fill them. I had also purchased a car upon arriving in L.A. after over six years on foot, bicycle, and public transit in Massachusetts. Feeling that I was losing control of myself when driving really frightened me and I had no idea what to do about it. I was coming from a mindset that held that a loss of control was the worst thing I could experience. Each disruption was very brief and in time they frightened me less and less – they were just things that happened. Earlier in the process I was close to panic when it could happen, while later I knew I would come out of it fine. I worked hard to continue life and my idea of myself that I'd carried for a long time, not sure if I should let these experiences mean much.

San Francisco

For Labor Day weekend of 2004, I went with my friends/neighbors to San Francisco to meet a friend of the man's who lived there and some of his friends. We stayed together in the home of the family for whom one of the women was a nanny, as the family was out of town. I felt at home with the San Francisco-Berkeley vibe they carried. One of them in particular stood out to me with her sensitivity and openness, and when she first saw me as we got to the front door, her look to me seemed to say, "Oh, *there* you are." I felt reconnected with an old friend after a long absence. This circle of friends had each in their own ways come to take healing and wholeness as important parts of life, and I was just getting there. A handful of them had over time a profound impact on shaking me out of my old, unhealthy habits and patterns, often in just being who they were as I learned about my own vibration contrasted with theirs.

The biggest (and to me almost crazy) idea that shook me from being around them was that health and happiness requires listening to the body as part of one's whole being, and caring for one's self as a whole being. When you live in your head you watch the things that happen in and on your body with detachment. You observe that something hurts or that you like the taste of this or that, but you might not be *in* your body – you don't always experience your body as you. These people were deeply attuned to the languages of their bodies and at first I felt out of my element and confused. I was pretty sure I was a clueless foreigner visiting a land I hadn't previously known even existed.

The three of us went back to San Francisco for Halloween and then again for Thanksgiving. At Thanksgiving I talked with another of their friends I had met only briefly on the previous trip and did a evolutionary astrology reading for her after dinner. She later told me that she had déjà vu the entire time, as well as that my body was screaming for my attention and she could tell that I didn't know how to listen to it or what to do. I felt at home with her and two others in that group so I returned several times over the following few months to spend time with them (they happened to share a house in Albany, on the edge of Berkeley). I loved how they were influencing me even as it made resistant parts of me uncomfortable. It felt good to be me when I was with them, something I wasn't all that familiar with. Between them, I had my first taste of a number of ideas about health, wellness, and healing modalities new to me that were already part of their lives. I tried to take cues from them even as parts of me were confused and others fought. I knew that I was being given some really great opportunities to stretch into new ways of being.

The strange psychic experiences continued to escalate. One of the women recommended I meet another friend of hers, thinking we might trade services before I went back to L.A. I would do a evolutionary astrology reading for her and she would channel my spirit guides for me. That trade took place on New Year's Eve day 2004. I felt that what I received through her was akin to marching orders from some part of me I didn't yet know anything about. It wasn't me but it was about me .. but it was me and for me – there were many layers in what went down and my radar went off, telling me something good was happening and that it was good. She brought through messages from my spirit guides and offered me imagery of what she saw when she looked into how my energy field was then operating and how my life was unfolding as a result. Observing her enter and work within her channeling mode was fascinating. Still sure that I was not the kind of person who did or would ever do things like that, I sensed the changes in consciousness she was experiencing and found myself intrigued. I thought that an energy had descended in the room, but it was in fact her consciousness shifting to pick up the frequencies on which guidance communicates. It changed how it felt to be in the room. You'll read more in the next chapter (*Awakened Spirit*) about that channel and what I learned from working with her in her class.

Returns

I was immersed in evolutionary astrology and had begun to see clients professionally by the time I moved to Santa Monica in late 2004. One day when I was getting some laundry out of my apartment complex's laundry room, my shoe got caught against a step and I was stuck still for a split second. I suddenly didn't understand what was going on, and then I heard me tell myself in a flash: *You moved to L.A., you do astrology now, these are your friends and what's happened here so far* (accompanied by a slide show of times with them from the previous year) – a run-down or briefing for a part of me that had suddenly returned.

The idea behind the shamanic practice of soul retrieval is that there are circumstances in life during which a part of a person can find it advantageous to split off and go somewhere else. This fragmentation can happen as a result of trauma, illness, or any source of intense stress including loss of loved ones, jobs, homes, and anything else important to us. The fragment of the person splits off so that he or she can be less conscious of the unpleasant or traumatic experience he or she is having. A shaman is trained to identify fragments that have departed, locate them, and bring them back. It is entirely possible for individuals to do this for themselves, yet having a shaman is the standard, traditional choice.[2]

Knowing only a bit about the idea of soul retrieval, I began experiencing it spontaneously that day. The part of me just returned was shocked that I had moved to California (it asked me if I was really the kind of person who would do that). As he got

---

[2] I have since learned effective methods from Ascended Master Djehuty (a.k.a. Thoth, St. Germain, and Merlin) to do retrieval work on oneself and regularly teach them to clients and students.

used to the idea, I kept thinking with a huge grin, "*I moved to California.*" I went back into the apartment from the laundry room and saw my roommate in the living room, reading. She looked familiar and strange at the same time. I said to her cautiously, "*I* moved to *California.*" She said without looking up, "You're like that, aren't you?" referring to my string of strange psychic experiences and resulting amusing behaviors. I then sat down to write a creative piece called "California," writing out as best I could the stream that had flashed across my mind when my foot got caught on the step.

Over the following 18 months or so, I experienced 12 more spontaneous returns of fragments of myself. Some returns were more dramatic than others, representing the return of a more significant part. During each there was a level of disorientation and then a quick and thorough briefing for the part that returned, followed by a snapping back into center or alignment. I became used to having them. It was kind of fun watching this shift in my consciousness happen suddenly and then watch it right itself because now I knew nothing was wrong and I was not in danger – I no longer felt that the experiment in which I found myself was entirely bad. After each piece's return I felt stronger, more alive, more present, more in my body and, as a result, more confident. I came to see that before the string of returns, I had been disconnected from myself. It became clear that I was far from practiced in any sort of connectedness, especially that of feeling fully in my body. This lead me to seek massage therapy and Rolfing in Santa Monica, sound healing sessions from an acquaintance in L.A., and a Rosen Method session with one of my friends in S.F. to support my increasing level of awareness of myself as a whole being.

Delicious Stranger

During this period I wrote down a lot of my nocturnal dreams after waking, recognizing that higher self, soul, and spirit guides can sometimes communicate more easily with us during dreams than in waking life. I had learned that maintaining an openness to right-brain realities is a skill to be developed in order to develop psychically. Writing your dreams down right after you wake brings a portion of the dream world into your waking life. Over time, it can make a difference to have that little bit brought in and in my experience, it really adds up. Since I was not always the most open person to other realties when conscious, dreams were a great way to get messages. Tracking and learning to understand those I could make sense out of became enjoyable, a game of sorts that I was learning to play as I learned the symbolic language that guides use and the subconscious is filled with.

One morning I had a particularly impactful dream, the meaning of which I could not fathom right away. In it I am at a party with a drink, standing around waiting for something to happen. I'm not sure I know anyone there or even anyone even *like* the people at the party. After a few minutes of watching others mingle and talk and feeling that I was waiting for something to happen, a woman whose face I could not see walked by me and whispered a single word in my ear. As she walked by, all I saw was her wryly smiling mouth as she whispered the word in passing. Her voice seemed divine, magical, and sparked something in the dreaming me. I knew in the dream as I heard this word that I'd been waiting my entire life to hear it and I woke myself up to write down the word. A few times over the next six months or so I looked for information on this word *mahat* but found nothing that made sense. What I found were some references to Theosophical Society texts, and these proved too dense for me to understand. My brain got foggy and dense when reading them. I knew the word was extremely significant, though, and resolved to trust that whenever I learned about it would be the right time. Being a Scorpio, I do like a good mystery!

One night in October of 2005 while house sitting for friends, I was reading Hart De Fouw and Robert Svoboda's *Light on Life*, a fantastic book about Jyotish (commonly though erroneously called Vedic astrology). In it, they offer a solid grounding in the philosophy behind the system and it was there that I found the definition of *mahat* that I had been looking for. In this schema of the universe, there is an all-encompassing being that wants to know itself, so it divides itself into portions. Awareness of that division is *mahat*, and is the state of consciousness that exists before it is manifest as individual consciousness. I took from this that reconnecting to a level of consciousness higher than that of my individual self was at least part of what I came here to do. The dream screamed meaningfulness, and I felt the beginning of a reconnection to spirit just from having had it! I felt that the delicious stranger who whispered the word was a spirit guide of mine, and I was excited and comforted by the contact.

I suspected that this particular guide was one I'd heard about from my channeling teacher when we were partnered for an exercise during class, as there was at times an odd number of students (more on that class in the next chapter). This particular guide I have known in various lives as humans, and have been head over heels for her every time we meet. She has chosen not to be incarnated while I'm alive this time in order to serve as a guide for me with the intention of inspiring me to open to spirit and the unseen realms. She knew that if she were incarnated, I would find her and that I would be distracted by the, let's say, earthly dynamics of passionate human relationships. As it happens, all the fragments that came back spontaneously over the 18-month period had been flying around looking for *her*! The sense of loss from not finding her in/as any of the women I'd met in my life led to these fragments going off in search of her. I suspected that a number of them had left when I was 7-8 years old, when I realized once and for all that my relationship with my father would never be what I wanted and needed it to be. Some of these fragments might have left then in order to search for the one person I always knew loved me unconditionally.

My channeling teacher told me in the reading during class involving this guide that she was seeing imagery of me floating around the Moon and searching, looking all over the surface of the globe and beyond for a particular woman. The teacher's main message to me in the reading was, "Stop looking! You're not going to find her. Get on with your life and know that she is one of your guides. Develop a relationship with her out of the body." While a number of those fragments had by that time returned, a very loud part of me was sad to hear that I wouldn't find her! I also became aware that in my romantic relationships to date I hadn't been fully present, always recognizing with a little deflation that the woman I was with was not the one I had always been looking for. It seemed to me that I had been checking each and every woman I met off the list as not that long-lost love, which blows my mind to consider even now. At the time of the reading from my teacher I had just begun a relationship with a wonderful woman and was committed to being present with her, and this reading helped me see how to do that for the duration we were together, and since that time I have had none of the same issues not being able to be present in relationships.

One of the things this guide does on my behalf is arrange relationships. When meeting someone seems particularly important, I can find her fingerprints on the situation. Guides can make deals with each other to help those they support learn their lessons and execute their intentions. All but one of my significant personal relationships since choosing this road I can see as her handiwork. There's a vibration to what she arranges and I've become sensitive enough to recognize her energetic signature when she's involved.

Breathing Class

For close to 6 months I attended on most Sundays a breathing class with a tantra teacher in L.A. My introduction to it was via a woman I met who had been going there, and she was energetically vibrating in amazing ways and I wanted to know if I could, too.[3]

The class reflected a community grown up around the teacher, a warm man who was in my mind a good teacher. This was (thankfully) not the tantra that you'd find discussed at cocktail parties or bars to try to pick up women, but the real deal. Tantra is about energy, and the breathing class was about learning to manage one's own energy and life force using breath and locks. He also shared tantric perspectives on sex and sexuality, as all this breath work should be brought to a partner to practice. I learned a lot in his class and some workshops that he offered, and the woman I was dating at the time (the one who lead me to the class) and I put a lot of the breathing techniques to good use.

My experiences in the class over those months taught me a lot about sensing and feeling unseen things and learning to trust my body and myself, yet there's a particular experience that stands out as worth sharing. I attended a workshop all about moving energy out of the body. We all run and collect energies all the time and this is normal, yet if we don't learn to move them out, they can build up and stagnate in our bodies. The first part of the

---

[3] This is also when I began to explore eating a raw diet. I met several people at that class who ate raw primal diets, and I wanted to vibrate with the same clarity they did.

workshop was a set of partner exercises. One person lay on the floor and did the breath taught to us while his or her partner moved around his or her body and touched or briefly massaged points here or there to help the energy move. It seemed to me that I was supposed to know where to go on my partner's body intuitively, but it was kind of a confusing experience. I wasn't sure I read my partner well, but she and the teacher seemed happy with what I was doing. At the end we did a meditation and then he turned on some hard rock and told us to dance, ending the workshop on a positive, high-energy note.

As I came back from the meditation and began to stand up, I did so very slowly. I couldn't move at normal speed. I was not quite in slow-motion mode but something like it. I felt tied to the ground, and knew that moving too fast would damage the connection. It felt beyond good. I had moved enough stagnant energy out of my body and system to have space to fill it with the energy of the Earth – the calm, stable, grounding energy of the planet itself. There was absolutely no way I could dance, or even move faster than I was. I stood up over the course of probably two minutes, and then just drank in the feeling of being aligned in a column of earth energy. The message in that moment from a guide of mine was, "See what happens when you move energy? This can be yours if you keep up this healing work." I felt I was in a box of the energy, a rectangle in which I fit.

The song playing was Led Zeppelin's *Kashmir*, one of my favorite songs of all time. The heavy beat and dense guitar chords matched and framed my feeling of being aligned perfectly within the column of energy. It was another experience of deep empowerment by taking in the energy that's waiting for each of us to work with, that of the Earth. Not many of us understand that the Earth even has an energy field, let alone one that we can draw from and rely on to feed us when we need support. Learning to work with it is foundational to how I teach intuitive skills development because orienting to and learning to work with the energy of the Earth is a major part of learning to work with your own energy.

Constellations

Family constellation therapy was developed by a German psychologist and former priest named Bert Hellinger (it is also known as Hellinger work). It involves a client with an issue to resolve and a facilitator trained to help resolve issues in a particular way. There is a group of people that offers to be a part of this healing process, called representatives. They are arranged, or constellated, in the room to reflect the energy dynamics of the client's family system. The facilitator then helps the representatives through the process of healing the dynamics until at the end, when the person representing the client switches places with him or her. The client is then re-entering a changed-for-the-better family dynamic.

As it might seem from that description, the work is holographic. Healing the energy dynamics as constellated in the room heals the energy in the family system. It is also holographic in that whatever part for which a representative is chosen, the situations in the client's or client's relative's life that is being represented resonate with what the representative is dealing with in his or her own life. For this reason, representatives as well as clients experience healing and the effects on everyone involved can be profound.

I had the good fortune to be invited to a session facilitated by a sensitive, wise practitioner. The woman who invited me was an astrologer acquaintance who had a gut instinct to invite me. In all, I participated in about a dozen meetings (with 2-3 constellations per meeting) run by this man in the span of a year. I had my own done, as well. I met some wonderful people during that year and felt part of a great healing community, as half or more of the people at any particular meeting were regulars. My experiences in and education from constellations were most certainly highlights of my time in Los Angeles.

The space in which this work takes place is known as "the field," the energetic matrix that connects us all. Regardless of intuitive or psychic ability and openness, the stories and emotions of those represented in a constellation became available to those participating in it. The issues brought up by the client are traced back to issues present in the family system, so there are many times when ancestors who pre-date the client's life are represented in the session.

For the first few months I was chosen repeatedly to represent several eldest male children who died young, whether as war heroes or in accidents. I also represented a number of cold, conflicted, distant, and sometimes abusive fathers and father figures. I took it all as cues about issues I might or might not be aware of in my own life and family history but that perhaps needed to be brought into conscious awareness and addressed. For those who died young, I interpreted being chosen repeatedly as reflective of the foundational fear I carried that "there wasn't enough time." Eventually I became aware of a death of mine in a past life that seemed to the man as though well before his time. He was a writer, and he died in an accident just as he was beginning to write material that was personally important to him. In meditation I "dialed back" to the moment of his death and saw that he was imprinted with the feeling that the accident prevented him from doing what was most important to him. At the end of his life, he adopted a belief that you can be taken out at any time the universe happens to feel like it,[4] and this is a belief that has bled through time and into my consciousness. For most of my life I had a feeling in the background that there just wasn't enough time. I felt I had to work as fast and hard as possible at anything I found to be important because it could all be taken away or disappear without warning. The constellations brought me to be aware of how this was working in my life and how, frankly, wound up and stressed out I was about time.

Representing the stern and cold father figures also made a lot of sense to me, given feelings I'd carried up to that point in life. Most of my life I'd been really hard on myself with a strong voice of judgment in play. Most of the harshness was directed toward myself, and these constellations gave me the opportunity to feel into the stories, emotions, and thoughts of other people sharing the same tendency. I had the chance to see from the inside out how it affected their lives, choices, and relationships, as well as their family systems down through history. It took me some time to learn the difference – to catch the voice of judgment and turn it into a voice of support – and ease out of that pattern, but it definitely has been

---

[4] This is not true, but some who die suddenly in the middle of works they find important can be imprinted with this. The truth is that a person dies when that life as a chapter in the soul's journey is complete.

worth it and the constellations showed me how to begin that process.

Being in the field during the constellations was an amazing experience for me even without those cues for my personal healing. I became sensitive enough to see the quanta of energetic information running through the system before they were named. A representative would have a feeling and I would feel as it arrived in his or her awareness, before even the person had any time to assimilate, react to, or verbalize it. As the facilitator was aware of and actively tended the group dynamics, I would see the revelations and surprises coming through the field as he did. An example story from a constellation would be something like a client stating a feeling that he was not loved by his parents as a child. Once the family members' representatives were constellated in the middle of the room, you might find the maternal grandparents turned away from a part of the room and the man's mother turned toward it (they are informed by the real family members' feelings and dynamics). A child lost in infancy or an abortion by the client's grandparents that his or her mother consciously knew nothing about could be the thing in the corner the grandparents can't bear to see. Yet their grief and refusal to deal with the pain of it keeps attention focused on an empty space, leaving the client's mother to feel it and long for it to be filled. That kind of thing would shape how the client's mother would treat loved ones and nurture her own kids, so going back generations in constellations can be fruitful for healing in the present moment. I became energetically sensitive within the field to the point that I could feel into and grasp things that came into it, such as the lost infant or abortion being the source of pain as soon as the people looking in different directions began doing so.

This was incredible to me. It taught me and reinforced the truth that all information is available if you know how to be open to learn it. The space created in the constellations for all the participants to enter consciously into the field was magical to me. I loved doing this historical-emotional archeology to help people understand themselves and their families better. To retrieve information during client readings now, I often tap into the field in the same way.

I have done constellation work with three other practitioners since that man stopped doing them, but the experiences were lackluster compared to the time with him. I suspect they were doing good work but I had been spoiled by working with a superb practitioner and one with whom I happened to jive well.

A Language of Symbols

When I arrived in Los Angeles I immersed myself in the study of astrology. I approached it as intellectual work and saw many great uses for it to help people understand themselves and their lives better. As my intuitive opening progressed, I kept being nudged by my guides to rely less on birth charts and more on – well, more on I didn't want to know what. In time I drew many intuitive types to me as clients and friends who told me I didn't need astrology charts to do good work with people and that eventually I wouldn't use them at all. In the beginning it made me uncomfortable because I didn't want to know about the unseen parts of life, and I knew that these statements referred to the things I didn't want to have to deal with. In time, my confidence grew and I recognized that they were right, but I still work with astrological birth charts. My understanding of astrology evolved over time to reflect what I was learning about the unseen realms, as is reflected in Chapter 4's section on channeling Thoth (a.k.a. Djehuty, St. Germain, and Merlin), which has been an interesting process I'm very glad to have gone through.

There was a particular day that I began to understand astrology as a symbolic language. It opened up the door to doing the multidimensional, karmic astrology I do today. I was doing a trade with a friend, listening to her tell me about her difficulties working through a situation in her relationship with her mother. Several times I went to her chart to see what they symbols had to say, but there was a moment when a guide of mine showed me the symbol Chiron in Taurus on the Midheaven in my mind's eye, and everything clicked into place. Chiron is about a wound, and Taurus indicates that the wound is about Venusian things including her value system and sexuality. The Midheaven represents our place in the world, how we would like to be or are perceived in the community or anywhere outside the home. It's a lot about what we need to be good at and respected for being and doing.

When I got the symbol flashed in my mind's eye, I saw that she had experiences in other lives and this one of being made an example in public because something about her sexuality has been considered to be socially deviant. In this life she is a lesbian, and is very comfortable with her natural sexuality. Yet her mother in this life had a hard edge that represented the kind of larger voices that determine what is socially deviant. While her mother was far from conservative, there was tension between them rooted in the ways that my friend was different from her mother. Seeing that some aspects of her relationship with her mother brought to life her karma of being told that she was unacceptable for being just who she is helped her see the point of the relationship as it related to her soul's journey.

For me, seeing the entire picture unfold in a moment from seeing one symbol in her chart multidimensionally blew my mind. My guides continued to plant particular symbols in my mind as answers to questions clients asked me until I got the hang of seeing the symbols in the way that they did. Once I did, I became able to answer any question someone brought me. This might sound an arrogant claim to some, but when one looks at the symbols in an astrological birth chart as multidimensional and representing energy and consciousness, one can see everything in a person's life in them. My style of astrology is now based upon reading the symbols in this way, and I receive wonderful feedback from clients about the particularly deep, sensitive, and relevant way issues are touched upon and addressed in their sessions. These days I can't see a birth chart without information from spirit guides and other unseen helpers becoming available, and for this reason I've developed clear boundaries regarding when I'm available to view someone's chart. For any of us a birth chart can and should be a map of that soul's journey in space-time, and yet when a person's intuition has been opened as mine has, it also becomes a link to the portion of Divine consciousness – or soul – that is that person.

2 Awakened Spirit

A few months after the trade with the channel in San Francisco, I thought to call her for another session. I contacted a mutual friend to track down her phone number and he told me she had moved to Los Angeles a couple of weeks earlier and gave me her website address. Her site had a listing for a channeling class called "Awakened Spirit" that was to begin a few days later, and I knew immediately it was for me. *Forget the reading!,* I thought, *I'll learn how to do it myself!* I remembered how good the energy felt when she read for me – how I had felt unseen things moving and shifting – and I wanted more of that. Her vibration felt right to me and I trusted it, and that was that. Two of my friends from San Francisco had taken the class when she lived there and told me that it would likely be an antidote to the psychic confusion I'd been experiencing since arriving in L.A. After so much confusion and muddiness over the previous year I couldn't *not* take it, now could I? I felt as though guided to just the right thing at the right time.

This chapter goes into some of my experiences in the course I took to learn to channel. I will go into several of the foundations of the course that can be applied to any process of learning to see through spiritual eyes – faith, discernment, boundaries, and symbolic sight.

Sixteen Weeks

There were in fact two courses, each eight weeks in duration and scheduled back-to-back. The second was an optional, advanced course for those who finished the first. We began as eight women and one man, and the second section began with I believe four of us and ended with two. The process was challenging, and some people opted to leave the class along the way, while others had scheduling issues and didn't take the second course or couldn't complete it.

Class itself included grounding, meditation, drawing to activate the right brain, learning to shift our perceptions about why things were happening and had happened in our lives (what I now call rewriting history), and partner exercises for intuitive development that progressed into channeling for each other. The first eight weeks were structured around the chakras, from 1st (root) to 7th (crown), and the second eight-week period took us deeper into the work and also into some advanced topics. The real work was between meetings in learning to see our lives and the world in new ways, what I now call *seeing through spiritual eyes*.

It turned out to be a tremendous amount of self-confrontation, and loud, cantankerous parts of me dreaded each and every minute of it! After I got wind at the first meeting about what would go down in each class, getting myself to the following 15 meetings was almost impossible. I was proud to be one of the two at the end given how deeply, thoroughly, and loudly much of me did not want to do it. The course was designed to lead us into a deep level of self-awareness so that we could understand more about the truths underlying our lives. The goal of the class was to teach the process of channeling, and yet spirit guides can communicate with us only via frequencies of love. The real work, therefore, was for each student to identify all the ways in which he or she was running a frequency other than love and to clear out any energetic patterns of fear that could get in the way of communicating with guidance. For anyone this involves confronting truths about him or herself and learning to turn critical inner voices to those of support and compassion.

We were given various tools for looking into our life histories to understand what unhealthy energies from the past we were still carrying and the beliefs they engender in us. We were also taught ways to work through them, centering on the approach to chakras outlined by Caroline Myss in her very useful book *Anatomy of the Spirit*. She shows the relationship of energy to health and how holding on to memories and false beliefs of various kinds leads to imbalances in our energy systems and, therefore, our health. This information can enable a person to see the links between attitudes and beliefs in his or her life to discern where there is energy leakage or depletion. The premise is that all leaks and depletion lead to physical illness because the physical body cannot help but conform to what is happening in the person's energy field. The approach is very empowering, yet there can be a learning curve for students who are very resistant to face themselves and their emotional and energetic blind spots.

We resist this kind of change because parts of us that have control over where our consciousness is directed in any given moment can be unwilling to give up that control. In any way that we have been hurt and it seems that someone else has caused it, a part of us decides to develop a strategy going forward to do whatever it takes to avoid being hurt again in the same way. We can come to identify with these parts of us if we were hurt so deeply or if the same painful scenarios keep happening and the survival strategy is employed on a regular basis.

My resistance was strong. It was centered in anger based in feeling disconnected from the spiritual side of life. I was afraid to find out that I was responsible for the circumstances of my life. I feared learning that I had a hand in creating all the things in my world that were less than pleasant. I was sure they had to do with a cruel universe or deity. In time I saw I had deep, ingrained beliefs that life didn't care about me or anyone, and all that happens in life is in truth pretty much a series of bad jokes on us all. Though I was teaching to my astrology clients and students that we have to take responsibility for our lives, turning the lens on myself was difficult. But I wasn't counseling and teaching people out of integrity, as it might seem. The beliefs were deep, and I was conscious of them only when confronted by difficult circumstances and when told by a friend or colleague to figure out why I would have created them. If you asked me about my basic belief system during this time, I would have responded with a sense of optimism and enthusiasm for life. I was consciously upbeat and subconsciously anything but. It took high levels of stress before those subconscious orientations could break through the surface to be seen clearly.

This is an important point: We can be consciously aligned with certain principles but when we un- or semiconsciously hold beliefs that counter them, we get in our own way. This is why I challenge people inspired by New Age teachings like those contained in "The Secret" but find them not working to engage in some personal emotional archaeology. The truth about the law of attraction is that while you *can* and *do* attract good things to you by intending it, you also can attract other things at the same time because of other vibrations in your energetic and emotional field. When you attract unpleasant things and want to stop doing so, you have to open to learn in what ways those other things are reflections of energies that you are at that moment carrying. Everything that comes to us is a reflection of our energy fields, so the solution to moving ahead into better ways of being is honesty about what our experiences and relationships are reflecting to us and then cleaning up our belief systems. It is then – and then only then – that we can uncover the incredible power each of us has as a divine creative being.

The class opened my eyes to how hard it can be to change one's beliefs and wrap up unfinished business from earlier chapters in life. It changed how I spoke to and approached my astrology clients, too. It gave me more insight into how we are not always aware that we are vibrating and broadcasting conflicting frequencies, and it helped me fine tune my awareness of the difference between fear and love. I also had to learn to identify not as some of my experiences or as the sum of them but as an energetic being having a human experience, and I was learning about how deeply karmic beliefs can be rooted in a person. "You are spirit having a human experience" is a phrase heard often in metaphysical circles yet I had to experience many confrontations with myself and numerous encounters with different forms of spiritual energy in order to fully grasp the truth of it. When I did so I felt that I had crossed a line and that all the hard work had finally begun to pay off. At this stage, my work with clients centers on how to help them get there, no matter what life issues they bring into their sessions with me.

In many ways, the process of the "Awakened Spirit" class continued for me for nearly five years. I learned that each person's process is different and that there's no benefit to judging how fast or slow someone progresses on his or her path. I also learned that the notion of progress can trip us up and that having expectations for one's own progress can have negative judgments built into them (e.g., the question in a person of what is the right speed for her growth can have woven into it self-judgment about how hard she is or is not working). Over those five years when I was up against some persistent issue that I first gained awareness of in class, I sometimes found myself thinking, "Didn't I *learn* this already? Didn't I already *take care* of this?!" But I needed certain experiences in order to bring home the teachings I'd learned and to accept that they had more truth in them than challenged parts of me had investment in maintaining the historical status quo. It was a no-man's land, an in-between stage during a transformative process, and I could at no point see what would get me to the end of it. I simply had to continue working with the lessons and truths I'd placed in front of myself.

Faith

There is skill in learning to see the truths of our lives. What is needed to take steps to deal with what we see is, however, something other than skill. Determination and honesty are important, but the bottom-line resource needed is faith. Faith underlines the entire process.

The kind called for is faith in one's self. Going through the process taught in the class, it became readily apparent to me after a few weeks that having faith in anything else in the world is a major way that we lead ourselves off the path of empowerment. Putting our faith in external things and situations (including relationships) will always lead us here and there – to good places and some not-fun places – but when we have faith in ourselves, little can shake us. Looking deeply into our own wounding and unhealthy belief patterns and taking responsibility for them might be the hardest thing we can undertake. When things get rough, we either develop more strength or give a little of it up. In the case of this kind of course of study, all of the areas in life in which a person is willing to surrender power – for any reason and to any sort of influence – are up for review. It covers all the bases and shows you all the dusty corners in your psychic attic that need be cleared out. Any and all weak spots in your energy system (and therefore life) will need to be addressed to remain present in the process.

When I was going through it, it was less than fun. The entire time, however, I remembered that I had gotten myself into it. I remembered that I trusted my gut instinct that I needed to take the course and I had a vision of what my life could look like if I kept going through the process. I'm not even sure I had much faith in myself to begin with (other than trusting my instinct, which was actually kind of new for me), but this was an opportunity to develop that faith by holding the vision I had of where I could get to and trusting the process that I had begun. I also had faith in the integrity and methods of the teacher, and felt blessed to have her guidance and leadership as I went through the process.

The more I believed in my ability to get to the other side of the no-man's land, the more support I received from my spirit guides. One of my friends from San Francisco went back to Ohio with me for me for a family visit, unsure why she was doing so. I didn't realize until we were there together how much I needed the support of someone I trusted. As I had been opening intuitively and psychically, I was more able at any given moment to pick up more energetic cues from those around me, which can mean absorbing emotions and energies that others are feeling. As with many on such a path, my family was living in their own ways, not having anything to do with the truths around which I was learning to shape my consciousness. My friend was much more sensitive to energy at that point than I was, and I could tell she felt weighted down by being there with me. It was important for me to see how she was affected by being in those environments so that I could see how I needed to make changes so I could handle being there with more grace and ease.

One night at my mom and stepfather's house, my friend told me what she really wanted to do with her life, her secret dream. She said she had told no one else before, and I was honored that she confided this deep personal truth to me. When the conversation was over, I went to our room to meditate for a few minutes. I sat down on the floor and wordlessly announced that what I really wanted to do with my life is to support people in uncovering their deepest, most secret dreams and support and encourage them to do whatever it takes to get to the place where they can live them. I was touched and inspired by the dream my friend had told me, and I stated this goal openly and with an open heart to the universe. I felt an immediate warm rush as an energy descended in the room on top of me, and I turned off the light and went to the bed to lie down. It was really strong, and caught me off guard. A handful of discarnate surgeon-like beings began pouring light into my 6th chakra – some sort of liquid-light goo – and this continued for about 40 minutes.

About 10 minutes into the process, as I lay blissed out while feeling this stuff pouring in, my friend came in and got ready to go to sleep. She got in bed and after a minute asked me with surprise if I knew what was happening. She could feel and see them working, but had come in not expecting to see anything and so just made ready to go to sleep. I said I knew something was happening and she proceeded to describe the scene with wonder in her voice. She thought that seeing this might have been the reason she had come with me to Ohio, as she was in the moment pretty sure she could no longer stay in integrity with herself by choosing not to see this sort of thing when happening around her (she'd been trying not to see some things in her life about her abilities and their implications[5]). She stayed awake with me and we chatted a little, as much as I could while feeling utterly high from this wonderful energy being poured into me.

The next day we flew back to L.A., and I had one of the worst sneezing fits of my life. I'd had many of

---

[5] As I understood it, seeing truth clearly can pressure one to live a life aligned with it, and she at that time resisting some of those elements of her journey.

them as I learned over the years about energies I could not handle – whether in the form of certain foods (sneezing is a normal response when your body rejects foods it can't deal with) or people and situations around which I found myself. After the intense sneezing stopped my nose wouldn't stop running the entire day – literally as though a faucet as we navigated the airports and airplanes – and my attitude was because of this sense of suffering notably less than stellar. In retrospect, I see that all the good stuff that was poured in through my 6th chakra could not help but displace lower-vibrating stuff that was already in there. My energy system was pushing out the negative energy that had been stored there and my physical body was disturbed as a result. Temporary physical reactions after energetic shifts are commonplace. As noted above, your physical body cannot help but conform to what's happening in your energy system, and in this kind of scenario the new energy needs to replace old and then get settled. [6]

The point of sharing this story at this spot in the book is that when you decide to have faith in yourself – your hopes, dreams, ambitions, and passions – you

---

[6] What I've seen the most of in this category is intestinal disturbances after solar plexus or 3rd chakra healings. That part of the body is a lot about soft organs, and the energy shifts can affect things noticeably when it comes to all the processes involved with digestion.

draw to you the support you need to make it happen. This is the law of attraction at work: *Supportive and helpful people, situations, and tools come to you when you are clear about what you want and you do not block it.* The higher you vibrate, the higher the vibration of what comes to you.

There is an element of intentionality and focus to the 6th chakra, and I was provided with support when I clearly stated a goal inspired by love. Loving vibrations are the grease for all spiritual wheels, and all intentions formed from and communicated via love are powerful intentions that move things in your life and the world. My intuition (a 6th chakra issue) was helped immensely by this experience, and I soon began incorporating my intuitive skills into my astrology work.

Discernment

In my mind, the general ability to discern is a hallmark of personal power. You know who you are (or how you vibrate) and have clarity about what is not you and not for you (or what vibrates differently than you). In the context of the channeling class, we learned to tell the different voices that were inside us from each other. There is a variety that could be in any person, from inner children to energy stored in chakras, from the energies of others we might have taken on or absorbed to the spirits of dead people looking to make contact and spirit guides offering messages.

Sometimes I think of this as an inner sound board, full of switches, knobs, and those sliding controller thingies. The process of discerning all of the information you have access to is akin to learning what each kind of switch, knob, etc., does, and then what each specific one does. In my experience, the frequencies over which all these kinds of energies broadcast are different. It took practice over time to learn to tell them apart with consistency but when an energy comes to me now it takes me just a few seconds to figure out what sort it is.

Inner Children

We often identify with our inner children. They carry voices of fear that have knee-jerk reactions to certain situations, thoughts, and possibilities. Such a part of us is formed when we experience something traumatic when young, thought what counts as traumatic differs between people and we process experiences differently at different ages. I find that most inner children making noise in my life and those of my clients tend to be younger than seven years of age. There are a couple of things that happen energetically around the age of seven that lead many of us to learn to begin developing boundaries – even if we don't do it in healthy ways – and to overcome some of the fears we had when younger[7]; it is a time of a shift in consciousness in children that sets the stage for later maturation.

The Energy of Others

At various times in our lives we take on energy from others. We may try to alleviate the suffering of a loved one or we could make promises to try to help a lover, a spouse, or someone else. Each of these examples can seem necessary or noble in the moment – each can seem an act of love – but each is a violation of our energetic health. That we deserve to and need to have clear and strong energetic boundaries and not take energies on from other people is not widely understood now, as we don't yet understand ourselves to be the energetic beings that we are. When we do grasp this – it has already begun to be seeded now and will only spread as we progress into the transition to the Aquarian Age – we will see just how important it is to clear ourselves of the energy of other people no matter the intention we had when taking it on. With a parent, for example, a 5-year old boy might see his mother drop something

---

[7] The 2nd or sacral chakra, which has much to do with our experience in relationships (we begin interacting with others as ourselves, not just members of our families) is first activated, and we have our first waxing Saturn square, when we begin to learn more about limitations and our place within the local worlds of which we are part.

on her foot and cry out in pain. He doesn't want her to be in pain and so he might make a promise to himself to never let her be in pain again or, perhaps, to do whatever he can to lessen her pain. Fast forward to when he's 14 and his maternal grandfather passes away, when he observes his mother descend into a deep grief. The child might still be energetically (though of course unconsciously) taking on his mother's pain. While it is 100% inappropriate and unhealthy, it can seem an act of love. Such a 14-year old would probably not be aware of any such vow from the age of 5 and the door to taking on energy from his mother would simply have been left open with his energetic consent but not his conscious awareness.

A couple of years into my process, I learned that I had done with this my own father. As a boy I recognized intuitively his unprocessed grief surrounding deaths of loved ones earlier in his life, and it hurt me to watch him feel so much pain. When I discerned that I was carry someone else's grief, I closed the door to my father's energy system and set about releasing it from my body. I had developed an identity surrounding what I was carrying on his behalf and had to learn to shed both the energy and the identity. It began with feeling the depression and despair that had grown out of his unprocessed grief and coming in time to believe it was mine. That was easy enough after spending years toting it around with me as if it were mine. With my clients I am always on the lookout for energies they carry and identify with, holding so closely to them that the energies from others seem as though belonging to my clients. This is a pervasive issue and we all need to learn to release all such energies. The meditation at the end of this book is a good place to start releasing the energies of others in a general way.

We can also pick up energy in our day-to-day routines from others. It can happen when we are vulnerable for any reason including depression, despair, grief, intoxication, and carelessness. If your energetic boundaries are not clear you can pick up stress, distress, fear, anger, and any other negative emotion from others. You know how a shiny, happy person can light up a room and leave you feeling great after he or she leaves? The inverse goes for those carrying negative energy, and we sometimes take it into our systems. There is also a situation that arises for highly intuitive or psychic people – whether they are aware of it or not – that might be referred to as the strength or brightness of their "light." The energy fields of such people can stand out among the rest of the population in the energetic eyes of spirits and humans who seek to raise their vibration by being around those who are "lighter." As the spirits of some deceased people are looking for contact – not yet knowing they are dead or feeling lonely – intuitive types can pick up special friends and guests now and then who really do not need to be there.

Intentionality is the key to establishing good boundaries, as nothing can happen to you energetically without your consent.[8] If you feel vulnerable for any reason, work on your sense of health and personal strength to make statements of what you *are* available for and *are* willing to experience.[9] If you know you have taken on someone else's energy for any reason, give it back! Do so not with anger or resentment but with neutrality because carrying it simply doesn't fit with the natural order of things: *it doesn't belong to you and it's none of your business*. That it has nothing to do with you is reason enough to let it go back to where it belongs!

There are times when energy that we take from others can be thought of as attachments. I have heard an absurd number of ridiculous stories about people paying lots of money to practitioners to remove their spirit attachments, which often doesn't even work. What each and every person needs to know is that an energy cannot stick to you if you do not give it permission to be in your space. Working on

---

[8] See below for a more detailed discussion of boundaries.

[9] Phrase all such statements in the positive. Re relationships, you might make yourself available for equality and open sharing. If you focus on not wanting inequality and walls between you and another, you will create them. Always focus on what it is that you do want.

developing and strengthening healthy boundaries will in 100% of cases lead you to being able to get rid of others' energies on your own. Use the meditation in the Appendix to begin strengthening yourself energetically. If you seek help from someone to remove any attachments you think you might have,[10] ensure that that person's motivation is aligned with love and be very clear about your intention and those of that person and make sure they line up together. In my experience, having someone do this for us doesn't last most of the time because the low energetic or spiritual immunity that leads to attachments is not healed by having someone else remove a particular attachment. We have to gain self-confidence and get rooted in the faith that we have the right to maintain our own energetic fields and live our lives in the ways that work best for us. If we have something removed from us without that self-confidence and faith, it's easy for something else to wander in to our spheres.

I don't share this with you to engender fear. But I want to make it clear that you are the "boss" of your world. What you say goes and if you are not sure you

---

[10] There is also a tendency to believe we have an attachment when we simply are not managing our energies in healthy ways or do not know what we are carrying, which means broadcasting. It can be easier to think someone else is to blame for the chaos and uncertainty we experience in our lives than to open to taking responsibility for ourselves and changing our lives.

have the right to be free of others' energies – whether they are loved ones in pain or those of the dead confused about how things work – you can find yourself wondering why you have to deal with the energies of others. The fact is that you don't but that your belief in your right to be free of those energies is everything.

Energy Stored in Chakras

This energy can fit into some of the other categories listed here, too. Essentially, it is energy that was either stored by you on some level for some reason in a particular place in your body. It can be an energy that resonates with a particular part of your own field and simply found its way there and stayed. Again, nothing can come to you and settle within you in this way without your energetic consent, so learning to set clear intentions about what you will experience with your energy field and life – as and after you clear yourself out – is how you can move ahead in healthy ways.

Sometimes our inner children seem to be located in one chakra or another. A common practice along the path of learning intuitive skills such as those discussed in this book is to scan the body from within a meditative space to see what in the body and being is calling out for attention. The voices of inner children are one kind of thing that can be found there. It could be that a part of you is hiding so as not to be found, or it could be that it is in a specific location in your body or energy system to draw your attention to that part of your body. Do everything you can to become sensitive to them and to learn to read them, as the fact that they are hanging out somewhere specific can be meaningful and open doors to healing their/your issues from the past.

Spirits of the Deceased

Many of us have the capacity to pick up on the messages of the dead. Before we know how to tell them apart from parts of us, they can seem like they are us. Before developing my mediumship skills, I practiced this awareness a few times by driving by cemeteries and watching the coming and going of the vibratory frequency of the cemeteries (there are a lot of spirits hanging out in them for various reasons). I wasn't there long enough to spend quality time with anyone but witnessed the passing vibrations.

It is time that we get over our fears about the spirits of the dead. We are ready for a heart-opening revolution to release our fears of death and how the way we live our lives affects us after death.[11] Many people have fears inculcated over millennia of religious conditioning that simply do not serve them – and are simply incorrect – and these have lead to

---

[11] See the channeled volume Conscious Living, Conscious Dying.

the fear-based development of mythologies about why we should fear those who are dead. The simple fact of the matter is that we need to live our own lives free of attachments by others and free of the energies of others. While we can learn from the spirits of the dead and they can learn from us, we never need be attached to them and dragging them around for any reason.

Spirit Guides

Communicating with our own spirit guides seems the most common motivation for learning to develop intuitive skills. It can be comforting to know that we have a team of beings ready and willing to help and support us. I believe each human being craves a connection to spirit in some form or other, as we know in our cells that we are more than physical machines housing mental computers. We sense deeply that we are part of something larger and many of us know in our bones that it is our right to know ourselves through a direct connection with the divine.

In whatever way spirit guides offer us messages, discerning the frequencies over which they are communicating is critical if we are to take in those messages. Information from guides comes to different people in different ways. Some will hear the guides' voices, some will see imagery, and some will have knowledge plopped into their minds' eyes by guides.

Others will be more attuned to seeing the influence of their guides in their day-to-day living, as situations and scenarios in their lives that reflect the messages of spirit, such as my relationship guide whose fingerprints I learned to recognize. Others will have meetings in their nocturnal dreams. Many people will experience a mix of these modes of communication and I fit into this category. In the beginning of the process of opening to these ways of being, the resistance my conscious self put up was formidable. I wrote down my dreams almost every morning for this reason, knowing that my sleeping/unconscious self was much more receptive to these other vibrations and frequencies. Chapter 4, *Channeling*, goes into detail about some of my experiences with my spirit guides and those of others.

Ascended Masters, Angels, and Aliens

Those in this category of energies tend to stand out among all the kinds of sources of information we might find running through our energy systems. Each of these frequencies is unique and unlike what we experience in our daily lives – even if we spend a lot of time hanging out with spirits of the deceased, nature spirits, and our spirit guides. My experiences with some beings in this category can be found in Chapter 4, *Channeling*.

When we can learn the different frequencies of each of these kinds of energy we can learn to clear from our systems those that don't belong to us. We can also intentionally work with other beings with whom we wish to interact or do work. The horror stories many have heard about all the reasons we should not channel are proven wrong with a little education and effort. I recently came across several people who told me that they were taught in their religious homes growing up or in classes for psychic development that channeling is bad. And since most people have a fear of death, dealing with the spirits of the deceased can have negative connotations. Some believe that you never know who it is that will come through, and therefore the danger is too great to do it at all. Well, we are in no way taught to have healthy energetic boundaries, and so of course people think that channeling and mediumship are dangerous! The truth is that when you are clear about what you're available to experience, your boundaries are strong and nothing else can come in. Sometimes beings who don't fit the invitations you send out come knocking, and at that point all you have to do is tell them you are not available. Again, nothing can happen to you without your energetic consent.

Boundaries

It is easy to think that boundaries have everything to do with other people. A common context for thinking and talking about boundaries is that there are certain things that others are not allowed to do to us. Many people think about boundaries only after they have been hurt, realizing as the incident happened that the other person was crossing a line – even if no one involved had any idea that a line had existed in the first place.

Seeing through our spiritual eyes involves understanding in what ways we create our realities around us through the energies we broadcast. We are each responsible for what happens in our lives. The spirit-informed way to think about boundaries is as those things for which we have made ourselves available. We might not consciously sign up for a particular experience or kind of relationship situation, but the only way it can happen to or around us is if we are *energetically* available for it. On a path like the one I have been traveling, a person will have to accept responsibility for all that happens in his or her life. Yet that person will also have to accept responsibility for everything that *has ever* happened in his or her life. Look at the things in your life that have been difficult and try on for size the idea that they happened because you were energetically available for them – even if not consciously available.

Most of us at least in some part of our lives are confused about boundaries. When we are kids we often take on the problems and pain of our parents and other family members, believing we can make things easier for them. It also happens in our friendships and love relationships as we can confuse who is responsible for what in terms of emotions, nurturing, and care. The word codependency is used a lot when it comes to this and it's important to grasp the truth that we are each responsible for ourselves – our lives, energy, and health. Each of us is creating the world around us to teach our souls what we are here to learn. All other people, as it happens, are reflecting to us what we need to learn. Sometimes that means that we have interactions with others that are less than fun. How we will understand these things determines what we get out of them. The meditation detailed in the Appendix is a great way to begin working on boundaries from the inside out by increasing your awareness of your energetic field and what is happening in it.

Like most people, I had a lot of work to do in my personal and family relationships when it came to boundaries. What I'd like to share here, thought, is my experience developing healthy energetic boundaries for use in public. Since arriving in L.A. and having the lid on my 7th chakra removed, there were many times I didn't want to have anything do with groups of people. I found crowds too stimulating to be around becaue there were so many stories and energies emanating and oozing out of people. As we have not yet learned what it means to be energetic beings, we tend to be careless in emitting and throwing our energies – emotions – around everywhere we go. As my ability to read energy was increasing, my susceptibility to being derailed from my personal agenda by the energy of others did, too. Learning the ins and outs of boundaries was a foundation of the channeling class, and so I decided to try some things out when in public.

At this time I lived in Santa Monica not far from the 3rd Street Promenade, a smorgasbord of tourist and shopping energy. Before I had learned much about boundaries, if I went there I'd shut down energetically so I wouldn't have to feel what a horde of random strangers in a public place was feeling. After I felt like I knew how to establish good boundaries, I would go to the Promenade and walk around in the crowds, practicing being aware of people's energies and the contours of their stories but neither taking them on nor allowing them to affect me. I was practicing being open to energy but being clear about for what I was available.

I made myself available to experience the energy as I walked around and to pick up some people's stories if the stories came through – but for informational purposes only. That was it. When I went there to walk around I focused on this intention and chose to believe that I could have the experience I intended, not feeling subject to the energy around me. The first few times it was really exciting and so I kept doing it. The effect after a few times was meditative. I felt connected to all these people in a generic but important way yet was not being pushed and pulled by their energies. I had some amazing weekend afternoons wandering around this part of Santa Monica, sampling the energies and learning to keep myself grounded and focused on what I was available to do and experience.

Boundaries figure prominently in the work I do today. Early in my practice a number of people asked me how I could work with people going through some of the hardest times in their lives and be as happy and energized about it as I was. They figured I would be drained from working on a regular basis with people going through difficult life circumstances. I explained about how I worked with boundaries and that what I made myself available for with clients was pretty specific: to help them, if I am able, see into and resolve their difficult life situations with clarity and for everyone's highest good. I am clear that taking on the energy of others is not healthy, and by setting the intention in my work the way I do, I ensure that I do for a client what I can do while maintaining my own health. It enables me to reflect to clients what they need to see and hear while I stay open and clear enough to sense into the truth of their situations to offer them clarity in the spirit of healing.

Symbolic Sight

Symbolic sight is defined as seeing a thing and the cause of the thing at the same time. Learning and using this skill figured prominently in the channeling course. I recommend that everyone learn it regardless of what his or her goals might be whether it comes to developing intuitive and psychic skills or just understanding life and how it unfolds. The basic premise is that everything has to do with energy. Everything that happens in your external life is a reflection of what is going on in your energy system. Just between you and me, this is the source for my work with people to change their karma whether we're talking relationship patterns, repeated traumas, money issues, chronic health situations, or anything else. It all comes down to energy, and whatever you're vibrating is what you are manifesting in your life.

A knowledge of the chakra system is important to symbolic sight. Our health issues are all rooted in energetic issues, and a firm grasp of the chakras enables us to see the links between our belief systems, chakras, health, and all everything in our lives.

Example 1: I recently did a mediumship session for a woman whose family energetically transmits to its young that life is hard. She had taken it on just as the others had, and the relationship she came in to work on was that with her recently deceased father. He had lived a perfect example of this energy and she was working to heal her relationship with him. I told her that the key to coming out of this hardness lay in committing to nurturing herself. Actually, the word I used was "babying" because I knew that with this hardness, acknowledging the softer side of her might be difficult, and that word might shock her into listening by challenging her preconceived notions. I told her to focus on all the small, day-to-day needs she recognized in herself. I saw that this would help her teach herself how to nurture in the ways her family did not. We discussed the symbolism of water as representative of the softness and flexibility that is the opposite of the family's hardness and as a basic daily need of each human.

During the session, my cat knocked over her water bottle, placed on the floor by her feet. I noticed it but didn't say anything because at the time I was bringing through information from her father. After the session was over and she had gone, she came back to get the water bottle she had forgotten. The ideas of nurturing, treating herself with softness, and paying attention to those basic needs was new to her.

Leaving her water bottle behind was symbolic that it is not habit for her to pay attention to those needs.

Example 2: I worked with a woman who had numerous issues with her feet, legs, and hips. She was in physical therapy for them but felt very weak. These parts of the body are where root chakra imbalances manifest, so I worked with her on her feelings about the material resources she did and did not receive from her family. Years earlier, some of her family members had sold heirloom items when they needed money and had kept it secret from her, which upset her deeply when she found out. She worked on her emotions surrounding it and noticed an improvement in her strength with marked results at physical therapy. She asked me for the next layer of it, and I sent her on her way with the instruction to work next on her feelings about how women are treated by the religion in which she was raised, another root-chakra issue because religious conditioning is often handed down through families.

The issue was not being to stand on her own two feet, so I went with the things and attitudes she inherited (or didn't) from her family. The symbolism could instead have been about not being able to walk, which might have lead me to take things in another direction. From within the meditative space created by the meditation included in the Appendix, it was clear to me which energetic statement was being made by her energy system that were coming out as these health issues. I felt one vibrate higher or faster because I was deeply attuned to what she was carrying, open to the possibility that would lead to healing.

Example 3: I know a woman with a 7-year old son who has asthma and allergy issues. There has always been a lot of tension between his parents – a lot of love, but also a lot of discord. His asthma is due to his energetic unwillingness to breathe in the energies that surround him. The allergies are due to his feeling that he's not safe in life – allergies are immune system malfunctions – which stems from his not feeling safe at home because of the tension in the environment. Currently the boy takes prescription medications for these health issues, but it is my hope that someday his parents might be open to learning more about this perspective. Even if the tension between them continues, they have choices about how to work with their son on how to deal with his feeling of not being safe at home.

Example 4: I worked with a client who had intracranial hypertension, a situation in which there is too much liquid around the brain and the pressure builds up. She has had intense headaches from it for years. She knew that I use astrology and karma to get to the bottom of health issues and so asked me to look into her situation. I saw that energy was trying to get out of her head, and because of where it was, it was clear to me that she had major blocks keeping her crown or 7th chakra closed off. I believe that each person craves a direct connection with spirit in some form and that when we deny that urge for whatever reason, we can have various sorts of health issues. Her astrological birth chart told me that while she needed to have a direct connection to other worlds, she came from an intellectual family that might not know how to open to the spiritual side of life. She confirmed that this health issue runs in the family and after I gave her suggestions about working through this block and the beliefs associated with it, she was excited to work on it and relieved to have some tools to teach her children – some of whom also have the condition – how to do so. It made total sense to her and she felt great relief to have acknowledged that connecting to spirit was indeed an important part of life, which supported her in unwriting some of her family's conditioning.

Symbolic sight is used extensively by medical intuitives such as Caroline Myss and Louise Hay. I use it constantly and in all sorts of areas. It is the single most important tool in my intuitive tool box, supporting and informing everything I do. This is one reason I'm able to translate the karmic messages of an astrological birth chart into an understanding of present-day health issues and help people turn each around by altering how their energy systems are functioning. It is powerful.

In addition to use in work, I use it in my personal life all the time. When I'm drawing a lot of one kind of interaction or person to me, I look at the energetic statement behind the situations to see what they represent in my life that needs attention. For example, I might draw a lot of praise for my work in a particular week to show me that I'm not appreciating myself. Or I might draw people not saying what they mean if I'm for some reason not telling someone in my life something important.

Summary

While my formal channeling classes lasted four months, I was in the laboratory portion for about five years to learn the ins and outs of how to reorient my life. In retrospect, I am extremely grateful for having that class put in front of me when it was, and for all I learned about myself and life that the class began. I could not have known how I was to get to my goal, but continued to have faith that I would and as a result was supported in getting there.

After I completed the courses I sent four people to the teacher who ended up taking it, three clients and a girlfriend. All of them had asked me how I learned to work with my guides and that class was the answer. I've modeled my own intuitive skills development training on my experience in that class plus the five years of laboratory work that followed it.

3 Mediumship

I define mediumship as creating a bridge between the living and the dead. A medium – sometimes referred to as a psychic medium – relays messages back and forth, acting as an intermediary between the worlds or dimensions. Different mediums have different tools for doing this and no tool is better than any other. My primary tool is emotional information – which I put into words – and I also receive some thoughts and images from the dead while insight into their belief systems can seem to plop into my head.

As I've advertised myself a medium, I've heard a lot of negative opinions from people about that word. Some are uncomfortable with the prospect of hearing what I might say next while others are dismissive right off the bat. There's a long history of people calling themselves mediums taking advantage of people's trust when it comes to purporting to bringing through messages from the dead. Most references to mediumship in popular culture for a long time have been derisive or tongue-in-cheek, poking fun both at those who think they can fool others and those so willing to be fooled. Yet there's also a long history of people calling themselves mediums who have done wonderful work for others. The bottom line is that while there are many mediums doing good work, it is in many cultures' best interests to denounce mediums as frauds and swindlers. This is so because of how many cultures have been set up and have thrived during the Piscean Age, which has been in play on Earth for roughly the last 2,100 years. Members of these societies are supposed to listen to and follow the directions of those higher up in the social, economic, and religious food chains. Hierarchies and clear divisions of who gets what social, economic, and religious power when are paramount in the Piscean Age.

The religions of the Piscean Age (notably those of the Judeo-Christian variety) tell us that we need an intermediary between ourselves and divinity. These religions will thrive as long as we believe that this is true. Those who claim direct contact with God or angels are often treated with derision because they challenge the codified distillations and versions of truth about God and how the world works around which organized religions have been built. Some such people are of course canonized years after their deaths, with official opinions about them changed. Yet the treatment many receive in life – when they might seem to threaten the authority of religious powers – is often horrible. Acceptance by organized religions of the truth of people's experiences with spiritual forces outside their doctrine will be long in coming, if at all.

It is also true that many people have frightening experiences with spirits of different kinds. Children are remarkably open to metaphysical phenomena. When we are aware of spirits and open, we can attract them to us. They see our light on the switchboard as *on*; we're on their radar. Yet close contact with spirits of the deceased, angels, aliens, or anyone else noncorporeal can overwhelm any of us, especially children if they have been scared into thinking they should be afraid. Most of us do not know that we can say "no, thanks" to a visit from any of these kinds of beings, leaving even well-meaning discarnates seen and felt as dangerous. Spirit guides, ascended masters and many spirits or deceased people will be sensitive to what a person can and cannot handle, yet there are those spirits of the deceased and some other beings who, for different reasons, might not.

It's time to let all of this fear and trepidation go, as the work of mediums is so important to the healing and spiritual evolution of life on the planet.

Discarnate Spirits of Humans

When a person dies, the spirit is separated from the body, in a way similar to how we have seen this depicted on television and in movies: the lifeless body remains where it is and the conscious and energy field of the individual separates from it. If the spirit is open to seeing it, a door can open to "the light" – also as we've seen depicted in popular media. If the spirit is open to it, loved ones who died before him or her will be seen to be waiting to welcome him or her from within the light. There is a process of orientation those loved ones and one's spirit guides help to happen if the newly deceased individual is open to it. It involves getting the bird's eye or spiritual view on why the person's life unfolded in the ways it did. A spirit will see what it thought was happening when it as a human made certain choices, and it will see the spiritual truth behind choices made. Also apparent become the point and purposes of each and every major relationship of the person's life. Karmic connections and metaphysical dynamics not apparent during life are revealed, and the spirit of the person has the opportunity to open to the truth of what happened and why certain choices seemed better than others. Taking in these truths can result in healing and releasing all the judgments, resentments, prejudices, biases, guilt, and shame collected about the world and individuals in one's human life.

These are all opportunities the newly deceased can choose to experience. He or she can open to them or not do so and there is absolutely no external pressure to do so. Some are full of resistance to learning what's offered to them and others are not. For those who are open, they get on with their orientation. Those who are not open simply remain within the beginning stage of orientation for as long as they need to do so. There is no time in the dimension in which they exist, but months and years and longer can pass in human time before they open to change. They can during this time observe those who have survived them, and have awareness of the role model-type examples offered by their deceased loved ones who have been helping them transition to this phase of existence.

Change, of course, requires a willingness to give up attitudes and ideas of self, the world, and others in one's life, as well as life itself. Essentially, what happens is that upon being welcomed into the light, a spirit is given the chance to change his or her mind about many of the happenings in and relationships of the most recent human life by learning the truths behind things. Let's take the example of a man who had a combative relationship with his sister. He will be shown the overarching story of his and her lives separately, and how the lives of each fit in with the journeys of their souls. The karmic basis of their relationship – what was on the table to be resolved between them – will be shown to him. Let's say the karma centers on a rivalry for validation from their parents or being in competition for affection from them or gaining status within the family. During life perhaps he thought that she didn't deserve the same treatment as he did, and so he resented her. He might be shown that the karmic lesson they as souls have agreed to teach each other is to learn to love each other in ways that each perceives he or she was not loved by their parents and other family members. Perhaps in other lives they are business rivals or spouses who resent each other or any number of other possible relationships in which competition can be a factor. He can then choose to accept this bird's-eye view as true over what he while living *thought* was true, or he can remain committed to the belief about her worth he developed and attached himself to during his life.

From the human perspective – in which conceptions of progress and responsibility can be highly valued – it might be easy to judge this: *He has seen the truth, after all, right? Who does he think he is to deny the real story and cling to his small-minded beliefs?*

The soul's journey through many lives for each of us centers on our exercise of free will. Each of us has free will at every step of the way – including after death when we are exposed to all sorts of wonderful truths. And here is an important point: There is no judgment for those who do not open to new truths. I see the human spiritual journey as exploring what love is – what it means, where it comes from – everything about it. This includes how it is that we can love ourselves and others in the ways that others have seemed not to love us, and in this between-life phase we are greeted only with love. Whatever judgment we meet there is self-judgment, and its existence is one core truth of the human life experience that we all must learn through and then learn to change. If we have not done so at any other time, after we pass away and are in this orientation phase we have to face our interest and investment in self-judgment.

There are elements of our personalities that remain with us after we cross over. Those who open to accepting the bird's-eye view of and truths about their lives, experiences, and relationships grow beyond the need to be right about the beliefs and attitudes they held during life. All that could be viewed as divisive and petty in an individual is what can be overcome and released during the process of accepting the truth of things.

It is not uncommon for the spirit of a deceased person to return to make contact with his or her surviving loved ones to apologize for what was done or not done during life that created difficulty, pain, and rifts between them. These spirits can see the benefit of resolving old, unfinished business with loved ones. They have learned that no matter the difficulties accrued and built up between people during life, showing our love for each other above everything else is not just healing but the balm for everything that goes wrong between people. These spirits have learned the truth that the only reason we incarnate in family groups together – and marry each other and be each other's children, parents, and siblings again and again – is because of love. The karmic basis for all of our relationships is, in fact, love. If we didn't love each other, we would not agree to be teachers for each other at the level of spirit and soul, which we all do for one another over and over again in many lives together.

All of this so far has been about the process as it normally works, but it doesn't always work that way. Just as individuals are unique and complex, so are the journeys of their souls. There are three important categories of spirits of the deceased that do not fit with the story above, and their situations deserve exploration.

The Unaware

The first category includes those who are not aware that they have passed away. Trauma figures prevalently in many of these deaths, though there are other factors that can put one in this group. With trauma, the suddenness of death can leave one stuck in a moment of shock about just what it is that has happened. For others, dying peacefully in their sleep might in a way go unnoticed by them! They might simply perceive that they wake up in the morning and go about their business, not noticing right away that anything had changed.

For those traumatized or otherwise not knowing that they are dead, they can stay where they lived or they can wander. Many of them try to get the attention of the living, and this is a main source of stories about homes and other places being haunted. We've been lead to believe through various popular media that when this happens there is probably malicious intent behind it. This draws on the sensationalist fears we have about the dead and otherworldly others, ultimately trying to teach that we actually *should* be afraid of them. But this is just not true. The work I've done at houses which are occupied by spirits – often an unhappy experience for those who at the time live there – has shown me that most are benign and simply trying to make contact and figure out what is going on. They don't know where to go or what to do, so they stick around living people in hopes of being able to make contact.

It takes a tremendous amount of energy for such spirits to move objects in the space-time dimension or open or knock on doors (or hide or unhide things, etc.). For every time there's such an action taken, we can safely assume there have been dozens of times that the spirit has attempted to make energetic or spiritual contact with the human parties. Most of us are living in preoccupation with our thoughts, plans, intentions, worries, and histories. Most of us are therefore not open to or available to experience the existence of other dimensions, and why should we? We live here and now and all that other stuff is probably nonsense anyway, right? When a spirit makes contact with someone living in this mode it can be traumatic for the living. A good medium can facilitate communication between the two and support a resolution to the situation amenable to both parties.

Those who wander often seek to find people who will interact with them. They do not understand – and in fact cannot conceive of – why everyone would ignore them. This can be very frightening and painful. They might wander down the street or travel great distances and settle somewhere new. The feelings of displacement and loneliness can be strong in them. They will tend to be drawn toward people whose energetic lights are bright, whether those people are aware of their intuitive and psychic skills or not.

For the dead who do not yet know that they have passed away, they need to be made aware of it but with sensitivity. They may turn out to have attachments to things, people, and places in life that they need support in choosing and seeing how to release. Those who accept the truth of what they're being told will need to resolve issues with some of their living loved ones in order to feel ready to move on. If you didn't know that you died – if it was sudden or in your sleep – you wouldn't have been able to prepare in any way for whatever might come next. When I do this kind of work, called spiritual counseling, once a spirit accepts what has happened – which doesn't always happen right away – I explain that what can happen next can occur when they are ready for it. I tell them that they have loved ones waiting to welcome them to the next phase of their journeys. I tell them if they want to see them, to look toward a door that will in a moment open.[12] At this point I've already asked his or her deceased loved ones and guides who are willing to come forward and welcome the person to come to the door. When they do – and they always do! – the spirit yet to cross can see them if he or she is open. I love this part of the process because the fear and loneliness in the spirit can melt away in a moment, bringing their entire

---

[12] It happened that in some of my earlier experiences as a medium I saw a door open to the light, and it remains a useful image. There's no rule that it has to be a door and for other mediums no door might be involved, but I find it useful to convey to the deceased spirit that we're talking about a separate place.

energetic signature to shift into a loving mode and this feels great to everyone involved. Again, not each is ready. But now each has a conception of what is going on and what can come next when he or she is ready.

The Disbelieving

Another category of those who haven't yet crossed over into the light and their next phase includes those who don't believe that such a light or place exists or that, if does or might, they wouldn't deserve it or know how to get there.

Many factors can inspire these beliefs. A person could be raised in a religious environment of which teachings about heaven and hell are a part, but that person could leave the fold or for any number of reasons cease to believe in the religion's teachings. Some are atheists during life and some are not but simply do not believe in any sort of afterlife. Other have lost faith in the idea of a higher power or that one would be benevolent or a positive, loving influence guiding the course of the Universe. A large number of people live in their heads and their ideas of what is happening are what define their expectations and willingness, with faith in some sort of afterlife seeming useless or silly to their minds.

Many people carry deep, strong guilt about what they did in life that God or whomever else who is keeping score surely has them down on the "no good" list for having done. Some of us are taught via religion that someone is keeping score about how we behave and even if we're not religious, our capacity for self-acceptance can be damaged with judgments about how we have lived our lives. There are many misunderstandings about the nature of karma and lots of people imagine that divine justice follows the same sorts of parameters of human, social justice (i.e., if I hurt you then I have to pay for it, etc.).

There are innumerable choices humans have to make in the normal course of living that can inspire deep feelings of regret, self-judgment, and self-hatred. Some people give their children up for adoption and some have abortions. Some people kill others. Some lie to their loved ones. There are people who cheat on their spouses. Some steal or stick needles in their arms and snort illegial substances they know do them harm. Some transgress the rules of their religions and societies and what they've been told God and the government want them to do.

The reasons someone does any of these things doesn't always compute with the feelings of guilt and shame that can accompany having done them. Soldiers kill with the sanction of their governments, but does that mean none of them feels anything about having killed? What about those who kill in self-defense or to save a loved one from being killed? What about people who steal food in order to survive? Obviously, killing is an extreme example. But doing anything in life against one's conscience, moral compass, societal laws, or religious doctrine or beliefs can inspire the kind of guilt and shame that may leave discarnate spirits thinking themselves not good enough to be accepted into the light. And again, the very visibility of the light depends entirely on the spirit's willingness to see it, so it is important for us to make sense of and peace with our histories while we are alive.[13]

Some of us witness horrors – whether in times of war, famine, or natural disaster – that make us believe there is no God or that God is hurtful, cruel, and perhaps even vengeful. The kind of meaninglessness that can result might keep spirits from being open to see the light, too. Counseling for spirits who do not believe there is something else to come after death involves supporting them in unwinding the beliefs they carried during life about life the afterlife, divinity, and the Universe. In my experience this kind of work often takes some noticeable time and effort on my part. The spirits have emotional attachments to the meanings they have attached to their actions, and the motivations behind them, just as do humans. To be clear, each and every one of them can work through these judgments and fears.

---

[13] See the channeled book *Conscious Living, Conscious Dying*.

Often, loving human support is what's needed to help them transition.

The Attached

Possessions, relationships, groups, places, and outcomes to which we are attached during life can be difficult to give up after death. The health and safety of loved ones, the disposition of one's assets, and communicating final wishes and sentiments are just a handful of reasons that can make spirits reluctant to cross over. Unresolved or unfinished business is a major contributor to a spirit's desire to stay on the Earth plane and interact with the living. There are also people whose perceived need for control is so over the top that they can't imagine letting go of anything even when dead.

Whatever a spirit is attached to, the only healthy way through things is to help him or her release it. It is not in the natural order of things to have spirits who have not crossed over wandering among the living[14] and unable to let go of what they were invested in while alve. The counseling for these spirits centers on, obviously, letting go. To do that involves accepting the truths behind why those

---

[14] Plenty of deceased spirits cross over and then return as spirit guides for living loved ones, yet this is a choice they have made and can happen only when they have opened to see their human lives through their spiritual eyes.

elements were in their lives in the first place. When the issue is relationships, learning about in what ways those other people were teachers along their soul journeys can lead to letting them go. All of our significant relationships reflect soul-level agreements in which we and others agree to be teachers for each other. Accepting the truth behind the human dynamic and finding gratitude for the support along the soul's journey is essential to moving on.

When a relationship goes sour, sometimes we have learned the lesson we set out to learn together and sometimes we have not. This is where a good medium can come in and help the living and the dead sort things out. Once each party understands the agreement behind the relationship, they can see in what ways they have been facing the lessons they agreed to bring to one another even as the human side of things made it seem they have not been working together or loving each other. Recognizing this and expressing gratitude to each other for what they have done for each other resolves the sense of unfinished business and the spirit can feel good about moving on.

With possessions, assets, and places, getting a new view on the symbolism of them in the person's life can open the door to letting them go. These are not often clung to for reasons of greediness but usually as representative of family history and connectedness, or perhaps security and safety and/or because they are reminiscent of happy, better times. When the emotional side of the experience with assets is understood, peace has a greater chance to be found.

Whatever the attachment, working with the spirit until he or she is ready to move on is the best thing to do. Real change for them comes from the inside out as they grasp more of the truths behind their lives, situations, and choices. Telling a spirit what needs to happen and instructing him or her to change, let go, or move on is neither helpful nor realistic. Counseling spirits in this way is the same as counseling people: until they grasp the truths behind things, they will not feel free to change. And at least in some ways, they still consider themselves human because they haven't transitioned into orientation. At the same time, when they *do* open to the truth of things, their ability to progress into understanding more about their true (spiritual) nature can happen quickly.

The living also have this capacity – to grasp quickly the truths behind the circumstances of their lives – yet it is so easy to be attached to one degree or another to our sense of individuality and our egoic selves that we can't always see this clearly or understand why we would want to. We usually keep our ideas of ourselves front and center and lead with them, and this makes it easy to keep our energetic selves at bay or, at least, to relate to ourselves in ways that don't fully support our energetic selves.

Some Mediumship Experiences

A Séance

A friend I knew from work ran a mediumship group. She knew I'd been on the path to develop my intuitive skills and knew I was channeling for clients and students, so she kindly invited me to join the group. It sounded interesting and so I agreed. Of the handful of my experiences with that group, I'll share one that covers a few different angles of mediumship.

We went to the home of a group member for a séance. The woman had been aware for years of the spirits that were in the house. She treated them more or less like a novelty or like old friends, which made me uneasy – it didn't seem right. We had come to do some spirit rescue and release – to help them cross over if that's what they wanted. The woman had lived with them for years and apparently had not tried to help them cross over, though I believed she had the ability to do so. The three women including the one living there set up in the kitchen with a glass on a table to do an old-school Victorian-style séance. The organizer of the group asked me to sit at the counter looking into the kitchen, as I was going to do some crowd control.

The house had been the home of a man who killed a number of women from the L.A. area in the

1940s and 1950s.[15] Most of them had been killed on the premises and these were the spirits we were there to help cross over. I was there, to the side of the action, to keep the spirit of the man who had killed them at bay so the other three could release any of the other spirits there who wanted to go. He had been intimidating them (still!), seeming to block the way out. The truth is that they could have gone in spite of this but they still believed he had power over them and should be feared. Everything in that dimension has to do with perception and so as long as they believed they could not leave, they could not. The organizer's idea in asking me to stand to the side and be the heavy was so that the others could communicate clearly with the spirits without his bullying getting in the way.

While they were getting ready, the woman who lived there told us some of the stories as she had learned them from the spirits. She seemed amused by the whole thing and happy to have us there to play. It frankly seemed a bit sick to me and I couldn't wait to get on with it. She walked to me and held out her hand and, without thinking, I took what she was offering. She handed me the key ring of the man who

---

[15] I did not research who it might have been or whom he killed. All of this information is from the woman who lived in the house and was familiar with the spirits combined with my observations and confirmations within the space of the séance.

had lived there, and it was my first experience of psychometry, receiving information about a person from touching an object belonging to him or her. His feelings of anger, hatred, and lack of control over himself flushed through me and it was horrible. I dropped the keys onto the counter, at this point convinced that this woman was bad news all around. I think she got a perverse pleasure from scaring me like that. To be fair, I'd never experienced psychometry but she had to know that I might pick up on his energy by taking the keys. Also to be fair, if I had been listening to my body, it would have told me not to take what she was offering. Yet because of that experience I at least knew what I would be dealing with when we opened the circle.

Just about everything I had learned about mediumship to that point was taught to me by my guides during the previous handful of meetings of this group that I had attended. We would do a group meditation at the opening of a meeting and set an intention, and my guides would show me what seemed brief video clips in my mind's eye of me doing what I would do and experience that evening. When the time came I would do what I'd been shown and *voila!*, I would have that skill under my belt. This made no sense to and threatened some others in the group who had worked hard over time to develop their skills. I have no idea why this learning process was set up like this for me, but I am grateful for these downloads that allowed me to progress into advanced work so quickly. As I think of that instantaneous process, it was pretty much the exact opposite of my experience with channeling, which took time and effort to orient to new ways of being. I spent several years opening fully to channel while it took a handful of months to learn what I needed to learn to be a medium.

We opened up the séance. They were using the glass to get confirmation of whether there were spirits responding to us, but I could feel those that came to us to communicate. The first was a woman who had been wandering that neighborhood for over a hundred years. I felt she was Victorian from how she spoke, and one of the other mediums described her clothing and it confirmed it. The spirit was upset about being unable to find a child, probably hers. She didn't know she was dead and was brought up to speed about her situation by the ladies in the circle and offered the chance to cross over. I cannot remember what ended up happening with her because the emphasis shifted to the reason we had come there in the first place: When we were talking with her, the spirit of one of the women who had been killed there came forward. When she did, the spirit of the man who had killed her came forward and I had to start doing my job as "crowd control."

Until I was doing it, I had zero idea *how* I would do it. My experiences as a medium so far had shown me that I was taken care of in that world and I knew I would be shown what needed to be done and how to do it. When we realized that the second female spirit was there and the man who had lived there was also there, I projected the intention to keep him to the side so they could work. A moment later I sensed a group of helpers backing me up. I looked over my shoulders and saw that I was the point of a triangle of these sort of grey, faceless warriors arranged like bowling pins. There were well over a hundred of them. They were lined up behind me like I was in charge! I took it as one more wonderful surprise and ran with it. I sensed that they knew me and that this was not the first time they had backed me up in the spirit world when I needed to do some work like this.

To my mind, they were the ones holding the spirit of the man to the side. Yet it seemed that they were doing so and *could* do so only because *I* intended it to be done. Their level of support was proportional to the strength of will I was focusing on the task at hand. I/We held him off, and at times he was threatening me and yelling at everyone else. Four of the five spirits of the women he had been intimidating chose to cross over after the three mediums in the circle explained to them what was going on and that they and they alone had the choice about whether to cross or not. For those couple of dozen minutes, they were able to interact with the other mediums without fear and it was definitely a good deed to have done that circle.

It is not in the natural order of things to have spirits hanging around. Any time one is identified hanging around, the only appropriate course of action is to talk with that spirit to see where he or she is in the process of preparing to cross over and to help the spirit learn about his or her options if not yet crossed over. Any mediums you find who are curators in afterlife freak shows or amusement park-style attractions are doing a disservice to those spirits as well as to the planet as a whole and all of life. The soul's journey and its healing are not matters by which to gain amusement and profit.

I was a bit overwhelmed when all was said and done. I felt that I had done good work but was not accustomed to the effects on my mind and body that working in that way could have. On the way home I stopped at a diner to have a heavy meal in an attempt to slow my energy field down. The feeling of being untethered to my body – including a bit of disorientation, inability to calm down, and my mind working so fast I couldn't think clearly – I know now was the result of opening myself up to do that intense work without really knowing how to be grounded in the right ways. Since then I have learned how to do this – to prepare for anything by getting deeply grounded to the Earth and taking the energy of the Earth into my body – but that night, I felt a mess. My meal did slow me down by, essentially, lowering my vibration. While all I knew to do in that situation, it didn't end up feeling good to eat such heavy food and I chalked it up to being in the process of learning more about managing my energy field as I worked in the spirit realm in new ways. Food can be a tool – if used wisely and consciously – to modulate vibratory states as we learn to work with higher and more intense energies, and it is not difficult to make some missteps along the way!

A Spirit Release

One Sunday morning my girlfriend at the time asked me to drop her off at an event in West L.A. We set off from our home in Venice like any two humans in a car would. About a mile from home, she turned to me and said something was off and asked me did I notice it? I felt into it and I agreed, and she said she thought we weren't going to end up where she thought she was going. I asked her if she knew what was going to happen instead. She was listening intently to the energy of the ethers. I was really curious but also driving, so I let her navigate us. *Turn left ... here ...* was followed by *Go straight three blocks no ... two blocks, then make a ... right.* This sometimes convoluted and circular process got us to a particular corner in a residential neighborhood in West L.A. where we knew it was time to stop.

We parked, got out, and walked a few dozen steps while feeling things out. We sat on a tree lawn and scanned the neighborhood, open to what might be trying to communicate with us. After a couple of minutes I identified a spirit in a house on the corner across the street. My girlfriend was beginning to learn to work with and trust her strong intuitive abilities and I saw that this would be a good opportunity to expose her to spirit release. I lead her in the meditation I did at that point to enter into communication with spirit and walked her through what we were going to do before addressing the spirit in the house. It was a lesson that described a number of the principles outlined above about the spirits of the dead and how it is best to approach, communicate with, and help them if help should be offered.

The spirit was of an elderly widow whose husband had built the house. She had kind of figured out that she was dead but was unwilling to give up the house in which she and her husband had lived their lives together. It was the last thing she had of him and, even though dead, couldn't see how to let it go to the "slob" (her word) who was living there. This person was a pack rat, evidently being influenced strongly by the spirit's energy of refusing to let go. I explained to the widow that there was no way to go back to the way things had been. After a lot of reasonable talk from me it became evident that she knew all this and simply didn't want to leave. I told her that she could be with her husband again if she were to cross over, and also that it wasn't right to hang out in and interfere with what was at that point someone else's house. I asked her to be honest about the effect she was having on the man who lived there and now owned it. Once she had heard all I could say on the subject, we left her to make the choice to cross when she was ready to do so. It felt like we what we were drawn there to do was complete, so we went home.

Two Client Sessions

Here are stories of two astrological readings for clients that included some unexpected mediumship. The first was for a woman whose reason for having a reading has completely vacated my memory. I saw several indicators of intuitive or psychic inclinations at the same time that I could see her reluctance to trust these parts of her. (I remember in particular a Uranus-Moon conjunction in the 12th house.) I was getting nudges from her guides to help her see how to open to listening to them, and then suddenly the room filled with a particular energy. Being very sensitive to energy, she felt it immediately, said she was dizzy, and expressed some fear.

I told her to send energetic cords from her root chakra down into the Earth and to breathe energy from the Earth up through them for as long as the energy was there. I told her it would help her keep calm. She did this and I put my attention on the energy. It was her late father, who had been struck by a car and died when she was 16 years old, almost 20 years prior. As you can imagine, there was some unfinished business between them. She had sensed him around her numerous times but nothing as strong as this. The main message he had for her was that he was a spirit guide available to her and that he would love to have a direct relationship with her if she wanted that, but she would have to be willing to live in connection to the other realms in order to do it. She left at the end of the reading happy and encouraged from knowing that she could have some control over how she experienced spiritual energy and could continue to have contact with her father. It is always empowering to learn of your spirit guides and have one rush in to offer full and total support of your mission.

The second client came in to talk about her relationships. She was separated from her husband, whom for some very important reasons she had realized was a poor choice for her. Since the separation she had been involved with a man with a pornography addiction, and another with whom there was a wonderful chemistry but the man expected her to take care of him financially. She looked at these patterns and knew there had to be a way to change things.

Her guides were showing me that inequality in relationship was a family inheritance passed down from generation to generation. I asked where her family is from and when she answered "Egypt," it all snapped into place. Her late paternal grandmother then showed up to answer some questions and offer guidance. Upon the grandmother's passing, her spirit in the orientation process saw the family karmic pattern that included abuse of women and resolved to help other family members stop it. The family had taken on the culturally-generated hatred of the feminine from that part of the world[16] and passed it down through generations of patriarchal culture, but to an extreme degree. The men of the family hated the feminine in themselves and did what they could to keep the women in the family down. That my client would attract inequality in her relationships was simply an outgrowth of this inheritance, as she picked up the energetic transmission from her family that women don't have relationships with equals and are not going to have the respect of men.

Her grandmother was committed to remaining a guide for her to help her to unwind her beliefs and behavior patterns about relating to men. My client took in my instructions about asking questions of her grandmother when she needed to and the various

---

[16] It is of course not unique to this area and of course not present in all who live and are from there.

ways that answers might come to her in response. She left the session feeling good about having made contact with her late grandmother, and encouraged that the pattern could indeed be changed.

4 Channeling

As with mediumship, there can be different definitions of what channeling is depending on whom is asked to define it. To me, channeling is bringing through the words and messages of other beings directly. If mediumship is creating a bridge between the worlds and relaying messages, channeling is giving a voice to beings from other places and dimensions in this one. The "Awakened Spirit" channeling class described above brought me close to channeling but my start with the real thing began following it. I was – you guessed it – resistant to the idea of opening up to let someone else speak through me. I wanted complete and utter control over me, my body, mind, and voice. *No one was going to get to use me for anything!* was the thinking.

My idea of channeling had been based in that of trance channeling, when a person gives over his or her consciousness to the entity being channeled. Edgar Cayce is a fantastic example of a this type of channel. When a channeling session of his ended, he was not aware of what had happened and what he had said. I sense that there was a partition inside him between his personality and his ability to bring through other beings and information. Given his personality and cultural/religious conditioning, this worked well for him. I was clear that this was not the sort of thing I wanted to do. As it turned out, I do a kind of channeling many call semiconscious channeling, though the term doesn't sit well with me because I'm totally conscious when doing it.

Inherent in my old idea of it was a fear that anyone could come in and speak through me if I opened the door and was willing to surrender myself to it. Since then I have learned that clear intentions about the kind of work one will do and what kind of beings one is available to bring through are critical factors in determining who comes through and the kind of experience one has. The spirit or psychic world is not a place to be afraid of if you are clear about your boundaries, and I hope all of us can get better with our boundaries so that we are clear that there is nothing to fear from doing this kind of work. For this reason, when people come to me with unfocused or undeveloped intuitive skills, I work on helping them see in what ways their energetic boundaries might not be in place or might be less than strong. This is the core of the intuitive skills development course I teach and the intuitive coaching I offer clients, in fact. People come to me wanting to learn to communicate with their spirit guides and then learn that they have to clear out and clean up their own energy fields – including emotional history – in order to do so. Most are surprised to learn how the process really works, and I love seeing them gain the full perspective on how to get where they want to go.

Wherever in life there is a lack of understanding, there is probably also fear. As mentioned above, our Piscean Age-related conceptions of divinity and the spiritual side of life have grown up and around the cultural imperative that we need intermediaries in order to talk to God. God through that mindset is seen as powerful and humans are told they can be powerful if they follow God's rules. What the Piscean Age culture shapers have done, however, is steer us away from asking just who is this god to whom we are supposed to listen – and we have *let* them steer us in this direction. We have asked to be told what to do and who to be! Patriarchal versions of God build walls between divinity and the individual for reasons to do with political and economic gain, and it works if people believe that it is necessary. A major feature of Piscean Age psychology, however, is that everyone does better when they do as they are told and believe what they are told to believe. So, of course, many of us have listened – we have wanted to be the right sorts of people and so we have complied. As we shift into the transition to the Aquarian Age, it is the job of each individual to ask who this god is and, in fact, determine for him- or herself just what it is that he or she worships. Whatever external idea, person or group a person gives power to *will* in time be revealed to be disempowering – it cannot help but be so revealed as we adapt to learning about and incorporating into our lives the truths about how things truly work in the Universe.

For the last few thousand years we have been taught to give our power to know God over to others. We have allowed ourselves to be disconnected from a direct experience of divinity. To my mind, channeling is a natural antidote to such disconnection. A person's idea of what or who God is might need to change in order to open to the idea of channeling but this would be in many cases for the better. There are many beings – ranging from ascended masters to saints to angels to aliens – who can help us understand better and deeper our true, spiritual natures to unwind from any and all Piscean Age conditioning about the nature and place of God in our lives. I believe that the energetic shifts taking place on the planet now that culminated at the end of the Mayan Calendar (a.k.a. 2012) will open for some people doors into skills such as channeling. The result of this would not be a bunch of people running around shouting that they have God on the line but a bunch of people with bird's-eye views on themselves and life itself; people living more in tune with their natures as energetic beings.

The sections below explain what each kind of being is about and does while sharing some of my experiences channeling and working with them. I also include some experiences with beings that were more like encounters and not really channeling in which I received information or help of some kind but no one spoke through me to anyone else.

Spirit Guides

Each person has spirit guides available to support, help, and guide him or her. It could be a couple of them up to a large group. They can be deceased relatives and friends (and even pets!) who choose after their orientation periods to come back to help their loved ones – and these might serve as guides for several family members and others simultaneously – discarnate beings who have never lived human lives but help humans out as guides (including ascended masters and nature spirits), alien beings of one kind or another, and the spirits of people you have known in other lives but are not incarnate during this life of yours. This last category can include family members from your current or other family systems, teachers, mentors, friends, or anyone else with whom you might have had significant relationships in your souls' various lives.

A couple of years ago a new friend asked me about what spirit guides do and what how they help us. The image that came to me was that one thing they can do is read the manual of your life as designed by your soul. Unless you are highly intuitive and trust your intuitions strongly, you might not be able to read that manual.[17] Your guides can see what you came here to do and they hold the image of and vibration of your highest good to help you get it done. The guidance they offer is always based in love for you. Following the cultural education that spirits might do you harm, some might find it hard to believe that there are beings running around out there who are only about and bring nothing but love, but it's true.[18]

The other thing they do quite a lot of is arrange relationships and circumstances with the guides of other people to help you along your journey. Perhaps you have unresolved karma with a person or group of people and it is time to meet that person or group.

---

[17] Most of us cannot read our own, though evolutionary astrology in the right hands can do wonders for developing a vocabulary for it.

[18] This is why the process of learning discernment is so important. When we look inside ourselves and find any voice that is judging or disapproving, it is not the voice of a spirit guide. Unhealed inner children and the voices of others are primary sources of that judgment. We need to learn to deal with that while we learn to work with the loving supporters for our time on Earth.

Your spirit guides can arrange to direct you to the times and places where you can connect with them. This is the dense and complex feeling I had when meeting my L.A. friend's fiancé for the first time, described in the opening of this book. It was the right time and place for us to meet in this life so we could have the opportunity to resolve the karmic tension we carried into this life from other lives. You might be drawn to a particular class or workshop or for an unknown reason begin going to a grocery store a little out of your way, or even feel it's a good idea to get to familiar places via new routes. I recommend trusting your gut instinct on these matters because being drawn to a place for unknown reason might be your guides working "through your gut."

When you state an intention clearly and from a place of love, the Universe begins to conspire to help you make it happen. Your spirit guides are major players in this cosmic love conspiracy, helping you put yourself in the way of what you want. They can communicate with you, however, only when you choose to vibrate with loving thoughts and feelings. Working with them is a great way to train yourself to recognize all the thoughts and feelings you might carry and run on a regular basis that are sourced in the vibration of fear. In your most frustrated and angry moments, your guides might seem around you but silent. It's not that they choose to be unavailable or withhold contact and information because of a judgment that you're not being loving – it's no abandonment or punishment. They simply cannot connect with beings generating the energy of fear.

There is an idea in the (at least Western) collective consciousness that people are tested by spirit along their journeys. When work with guides feels like being tested, know that they are offering you the opportunity to make new and better choices for yourself. The conflict is in your own energy field – you are being presented with an opportunity to move beyond some limiting circumstance or belief. Your beliefs and fears about the directions in which you are growing are what manifest as the feeling of being tested. Resistance to opening to the spiritual side of life (including working with guides) is based in fear about what we believe we will have to give up in order to do it.[19] If any of us gave up the need to attempt to control things and lived our lives through our spiritual eyes – taking in the view of ourselves that our guides have and learning to open to what the manual of our lives says about us and who we are– we would leave behind our histories and any

---

[19] More often than not – the vast majority of the time – what we need to give up to progress along our journeys are things in our lives that don't serve us in healthy ways. We get attached to all manner of habits and routines and don't like to have to give up things that seem to be part of who we are. They are however simply behaviors and routines; they are not possibly representative of who we are.

identification we take from them. Each of us can do it yet most of us are in significant ways attached to identities that have grown up from and around our experiences. Prevalent examples of this are those who receive a lot of accolades and those who receive a lot of abuse. A woman receiving accolades for her achievements can take them to mean that she is terrific. She can value herself for what she does well because others value her for it. With enough such treatment, she will take at least some identity from it. A man who as a boy is hit by a parent can take it to mean that he is worthless. He can devalue himself because the parent does. With enough such treatment he will take at least some identity from it. Each person identifies as his or her history, and the attachment to those identities being true can run deep in each.

Spirit guides can be with you your whole life or they can come and go. It's very common over the course of your life to have what I think of as a rotating cast of characters as guides. Different guides do different things and in the chapters of your life as you grow and change, you need different kinds of support. The life lessons waiting for you to encounter in a given chapter of your life determine the make-up of your guidance team.

Another important side of the spirit guide story is that they have rich senses of humor. When you see life through spiritual eyes as spirit guides do, you watch the unfolding of human lives with love and compassion for the passions, dilemmas, and foibles that go hand in hand with the human journey. If a person is taking himself very seriously and through that mode is getting in his own way, his guides will emphasize the importance of lightening up and enjoying life. This can come through events, situations, and relationships that have a deep cache of irony. It can feel like jokes around him being at played at his expense, but the goal is to reveal how remembering to laugh is a vital tool in spiritual development and health. Many of us tend to take ourselves and our lives too seriously, failing to see the truth of who we are behind our names, experiences, possessions, and relationships.

Remember always that your spirit guides have nothing but love for you. Learn to take cues from them to remember to laugh and enjoy your journey. They want what you want – when you hold love in your heart – and they want to help you make it happen with grace and ease as you learn the spiritual lessons that you came as a human to Earth to learn. A healthy sense of humor – and sometimes a deep appreciation for the absurd – comes in handy along everyone's path to spiritual health and wholeness.

My experiences receiving information from my guides have been split between direct contact in meditation and nocturnal dreams, and indirectly in my daily living. I stay open in my day-to-day life for answers to the questions I pose to them and I've become aware of their handiwork in my life. Situations and people that come to me as answers to questions I've asked them set my radar off because they have a certain vibration to them. Now, I could not be sensitive enough to this energy to feel confident in this unless I had a regular meditative practice of some kind. A practice teaches you to know your own vibrations so you can discern the vibrations of others (as discussed in Chapter 2). I've had direct contact with a few of my guides over the years, and was able to get to know some features of their energies and the physical characteristics of how they appear to me.

There are times when I don't feel like meditating. I might be in a bad mood about something and not yet finished being irritated. I let these things run their courses because denial and stuffing things into psychic closets and basements is unhealthy. If I let my moods run their courses naturally and without judgment, they end up taking care of themselves pretty quickly. That way, I also learn more about the parts of me that don't like what the rest of me is up to. As a result, I am better positioned to work with them to get them on board with what I'm trying to get done. During these times, if my guides have a message to give me, they will find a way. It could come in a dream, or I might for no clear reason see the same billboard all over town for a few days – never having noticed it before – or it might come through a friend who calls to offer me some otherwise random-seeming piece of information or unsolicited support.

In counseling sessions with clients I often receive information from their spirit guides. Many of my clients have some suspicion of what they could be doing in their lives to be healthier and happier and so what comes through from their guides tends to be confirmation and validation of their suspicions. People often come in wanting messages from their guides but the way the guidance dynamic works, there are not often gleaming messages of hope they have to share. They are our day-to-day support team, and unless someone needs to be awakened out of some sort of spiritual slumber, the results are usually less dramatic than people seem to hope. The vast majority of the time, clients' guides come through me to give them specific tips and tricks to change how something is working in their lives. It seems like homework, and I always let my clients know that it can be useful to view the suggestions of guides not as work but as helping hints we can use to further our development. These days I also type out affirmations for clients directly from their guides and the ascended master I work with, as reprogramming the emissions of one's energy field with affirmations worded in the right ways is powerful work.

At the end of some readings, the client asks me if there's any special messages waiting to come through from their guides. Then I tell him or her that just about everything in the reading came from his or her guides! I think it can feel a letdown to some but the fact that there is a team waiting to assist and guide them I would expect to make them feel special. It often makes me feel great in my own life, but I'm used to how these relationships work and what my part in them really is. I think when people ask this they are hoping there is some loving message that is not centered upon them having to do homework. But the existence of those suggestions *is* the wonderful message from the guides! Humans sometimes want to hear simply and only that they are loved and supported, that they are safe. While guides have this message to give, they also want us to choose to become empowered enough to improve our lives through more self-love. They aren't going to tell us that we are safe. They will point out to us what holds us back from deciding for ourselves that we are safe.

In our popular mythology (including religions), the intervention of spiritual beings tends to be dramatic and highly significant when it occurs. When we learn to work with spirit guides, the definition of divine and what the divine can and will do that many carry are – hopefully – called into question. *You* are the powerful creator in your world. *You* are the one holding all the keys to your journey. Spirit guides are available to helps you steer yourself in the directions *you* choose, nothing more. Realize when you begin working with your guides that it is a divine partnership and that you are the one who is running the show. They will not do anything to or for you that you do not ask for with, of course, a loving intention. It can be helpful to think of them as wise counsel available to you but a group that will do nothing without your input and direction, as well as a group with a clear ethical code. Working with your guides in this way opens the door to spiritual maturity, when you no longer want or are waiting for someone else to do things for you but participate in your life as a conscious cocreator.

When I teach people to develop their intuitive skills and/or a relationship with their guides, the process does not often involve me channeling their guides for them. It usually centers on helping them fine-tune their awareness of their difficult or challenging life issues and how to deal with them effectively and maturely, as well as learning to discern the kinds of voices they carry in their energy fields already. There was one notable exception to this, however, when a student was particularly challenged in her process and e-mailed me to ask if some despondency and lack of hope was normal. I responded with an appropriately supportive and informative teacherly e-mail explaining why we experience those things along this kinds of journey.

When I reached the end of it, one of her guides stepped in and said, "Hey – write this, too."

I typed what he said, essentially an extension of what I'd written in my e-mail to her. Its vibration was dense, as is all channeled material. As it came through, it seemed that I was dictating an overseas call with a so-so connection. A few words came through at a time, and the process continued for a few minutes. I sensed the message was coming to a close when another being rushed in. It was a type of energy I'd never felt before and was distracted, knowing it was alien. As I moved through otherworldly circles the previous few years I recognized that I already had some level of knowledge about each sort of being I encountered, which I attributed to doing spiritual work of various kinds in past lives. Yet this was a frequency I'd never felt before – *ever.* I felt into the one writing through me and realized that he was the same. He had masked himself so I wouldn't be distracted. His colleague had simply rushed in without being aware of what was going on! His message ended with a note to my student to the effect that *Tom just been distracted by one of us and won't be able to concentrate any longer to keep bringing through any messages.* I was intrigued and excited, and wanted to spend more time with the beings, but they had gone. The one who spoke was a guide for my student. Where they were from I don't know and they didn't want me to know. I had to let it go but I'm still intensely curious about the whos and whys of it. Of course, my student *really* wanted to know who they were, especially because I felt clear that one was a guide of hers. I had no answers and told her she should also let it go and trust that if it is eventually to help her to know, she would find out in time.

Thoth, et al.

I became very good at asking my guides the right sorts of questions in the right sorts of ways. The more I asked and the more love was behind my questions, the more readily answers would come to me. They would come from dreams, from synchronistic meetings with people who just happened to know what I was asking about and could offer feedback or guidance, and in the form of people who embodied answers to my questions often in the form of clients: I'd ask to learn an unknown truth about Lilith, and my next seven clients would be women embodying that answer as Lilith figures. Eventually, however, to get the answers I sought, I had to spend more time in meditation. I didn't like formal meditation so I would incorporate elements of meditation into my daily life and saw a small percentage of the effect. I'd go about my business listening into the space available through meditation, and it was this way that I began channeling. In fact, instead of meditating I was fine-tuning my conscious awareness to include the sort of awareness gained from meditation.

I didn't know for a long time who the being was who was coming to me with wonderful new kinds of answers, but the answers were consistent and I knew without a doubt they were true – they carried a serious, grounded vibration of truth and that vibration only. The vibration was all business, and I came to become familiar with it over time. My questions were in large part about how to take karmic astrology to the next level: I wanted to know about how to understand the bigger picture of the astrological charts and clients I was working with and how the soul experiences its numerous human lives. At that point, my counseling work was revealing a lot about the relationship between their energy systems and their belief patterns and, in turn, how their lives and health were going as a result. The information coming from this unknown source was helping me put clients' lives into the context of the long-term, multilife journey of the soul, making me more and more excited over time to learn the truth behind these human lives we are living and believe we are.

I'll give you an idea of the questions I asked this being. The planet Pluto in evolutionary astrology represents to some the deepest desires and intentions of the soul and to others the soul's deepest wounding. I played with combining these two ideas over time, and as I worked with this being, he began to show me that Pluto on a deeper level represents how a soul goes about exploring the process of empowerment during its human lives.[20] Seeing this and the deeper levels of a few other symbols in the birth chart enabled me to open the karmic story of any birth chart within a couple of minutes – I felt like I'd hit the jackpot as far as curiosity and a hunger to learn the truth of things went. I was able to see that each person's soul journey is the same as any other person's – an energetic being learning to live in a physical plane like this one – and this opened doors into working with people to help them effect their basic human goals. My work began to make a noticeable difference in people's lives, and I was thrilled to be able to identify these deep soul-level issues and educate clients about what they were doing here and why it was going the way it was.

At the Learning Light Foundation in Anaheim, CA I came across a book called *The Rhythm of the Cosmic Pulse* by a channel named Sharon Shane. It had a particular vibration and I just *had* to take it from the shelf and start reading it right then and there. In the acknowledgements she thanks Thoth, St. Germain, and Paramahansa Yogananda, and that was enough – I knew I had to buy and read the book! I'd

---

[20] See *The Soul's Journey I: Astrology, Reincarnation, and Karma with a Medium and Channel* for a detailed exploration of these ideas.

felt drawn to the first two and had benefitted quite a lot from reading the memior of the third. The first half of it I knew intimately because I'd brought through the same information from the unnamed source I'd been working with. I realized that my special channeling source for the previous five years was Thoth (a.k.a. Djehuty, St. Germain, and Merlin). The instant I thought this he came through and said, "*Now* we can get down to business." He immediately showed me a diagram of the relationship between a soul and the lives it is living in the space-time dimension. To grasp it I needed a bit of a consciousness software upgrade, and I received it from him then. I grabbed my notebook and drew a 2D version of it, and was pretty much blown away by the feeling from the consciousness upgrade and from the material itself. The diagram appears in *The Soul's Journey I: Astrology, Reincarnation, and Karma with a Medium and Channel.*

It was a relief to know from whom I had received all that high-vibrating information. The part of me that doubted the veracity of this way of living was, with this experience, put to bed. I knew that once you channel a being you can call that frequency back again – I'd had this with another face of his, Merlin, not long before this – and it was empowering to feel not so alone in the Universe. My contact with people had been undergoing deep change with regard to the kinds I felt comfortable around and how much time I spent with others, and my ongoing process of developing healthier interpersonal boundaries. What parts of me were trying to get from and share with others was shifting.

The different faces of Thoth I think of as stations on a radio dial. The information that comes through each is in my experience tailored for different purposes. The being at root of all these frequencies has as his underlying goal supporting the unfoldment of the manifestation experiment, a.k.a. creation. He often refers to it as the Divine Plan. He is committed to its perfection and that of consciousness, which will happen when the divine Source knows itself fully. This will be the end of time, the end of creation – the end of everything. His role along the way is that of scribe, teacher, mediator, messenger, and translator, and he never takes sides. For this reason there are humans in some circles who believe and teach others that he is bad news. His neutrality is often viewed as a negative trait because he will support anyone in evolving their consciousness. Those who believe this fail to grasp his role and, therefore, of what frankly amazing services he is committed to providing. If someone works with him and decides for him- or herself that he's bad news, great. But avoiding working with beings because of fear will simply put one on the radar of beings who resonate with fear, and that is the type of being that will be readily available to play with you if you do that. I therefore recommend a very open mind combined with healthy radar and a ton of self-trust when going down this road. You always get to say "no, thanks" to whatever you don't like. Remember that nothing can happen to you without your energetic consent.

The station over which Thoth comes through has a no-nonsense, all-business, intellectual feel to it.[21] This channel is about the big picture, and always coming back to seeing the perfection in how things work – even the painful things that seem to make no sense to our human minds. As Thoth does not play sides, we can learn from him to understand all sides of an issue and understand the spiritual principles behind why things happen as they do. When we open to these perspectives, we lead ourselves into a level of spiritual maturity rare on the planet at this time. As we progress into the transition between the Piscean and Aquarian Ages, spiritual maturity is necessary to move to the next stage of human evolution. My work channeling what will happen with the end of the Mayan Calendar has revealed that the major opportunity waiting for individuals at that time and leading up to it is to learn to identify as the spiritual beings that we are over our usual identities based in experience and history. Thoth offers a

---

[21] Since this writing, I have channeled four books from this being using the name Djehuty. This is his Egyptian name.

perspective that can help us take ourselves to the next level as human beings.[22]

St. Germain

This face of the being is the keeper of the violet flame of forgiveness. Many in metaphysical circles are familiar with St. Germain and are taught to call on him and the violet flame on a regular basis. Forgiveness is a key to countless kinds of human difficulties and miseries, and I recommend that if you don't know about him or how to call on him, learn to do so.

My experiences channeling St. Germain center on work with clients whose primary block to healing and moving forward is their own self-judgment and self-criticism. When someone is carrying this, it is often taken on from someone else. Usually a family member or 20 are stuck in cycles of self-hatred and kids in families can, when very young, internalize their parents' and other family members' ways of seeing themselves. One way to get closer to the vibration of St. Germain in your daily life is to evaluate each thing you do with the criteria of whether it is motivated by fear or love. All the times

[22] My audio course "Chiron, 2012, and the Aquarian Age: The Key and How to Use It," based on this channeling, explores the next phase in human evolution in depth through the Chiron archetype.

you find the answer to be fear, choose to let it go and reframe your motivation to align with and operate from a place of love. The more you align with love and live your life from a place of love, the more you can open yourself to experiencing and working with St. Germain. You don't have to do anything like this in order to benefit from the violet flame (which can be called on at any time by anyone) but this kind of process can clear more space within you for the violet flame to do its profound healing.

Channeling St. Germain brings the energy of the violet flame through the person channeling it. It is the energy of total and utter compassionate love and forgiveness. When I bring it through, I feel a little like a saint! The client whose life journey needs this energy called forth for healing is usually amazed at being in a room filled with such unconditional love and acceptance. I help those people ground within the energy and tell them about how to call the energy forth for themselves. It's healing just to be in a room filled with this energy. Part of you knows with certainty that you can release the tension of self-hatred and self-judgment, and just be who you are. It can be incredibly freeing.

These experiences have taught me to actively remember to come back to the energy of compassion and forgiveness. Like everyone else, I need to remember it the most precisely when I forget it! We all need forgiveness for ourselves, and the most powerful and potent source is turned on when we choose it for ourselves. St. Germain is an ally along the journey of learning to love yourself and others more.

Merlin

I did not know much about Merlin outside the ubiquitous King Arthur mythos until I channeled him during a healing and counseling session. I had been told by my guides that I could develop a session of counseling combined with a tantric breathing exercise to support women in healing trust issues. It was presented to me as sexual healing though it should be understood that a tremendous amount of healing for our sexual selves can be undertaken with absolutely nothing to do with sex. Sex is about energy and our energy affects our beings in their entirety, and so healing issues surrounding our sexual selves and histories is critical to overall health. This session was designed to create a safe space in which a woman could explore trusting a man, and relaxing into herself – her natural sense of femininity – and be fully present in the company of man without pretense, walls, and conditional barriers. I would set clear boundaries and go into a meditative space to bring through the masculine principle so that the client could have a "container" into which to relax enough to connect with her feminine self. I was excited about this work, as sexual healing is one of the most important invitations on the planet at present.

This work would be for women who had experienced any sort of major trust-depleting interactions with men, and there are a lot of women out there with experiences that fit. My guides told me to begin offering it to people I trusted who might benefit from it so that I could learn how to structure and pace a session, and I did so. One evening with a group of friends in Venice one of my dear friends said she had been confronting in herself the tendency to be aggressive with men as a direct response to having been hurt sexually when a teenager. I offered to do that work with her to see if she could benefit, and she loved the idea. I went to her apartment later that week. I explained the ideas behind it and how it would unfold, and we set a boundary and intention that the session was for her healing. The session was to be two rounds of the breathing exercise separated by a counseling session.

We did the first round of breathing, which offers a chance for the client to gradually explore relaxing into the space of safe masculinity that I created. For someone who needs this work, she can be cautious and the process can be slow and awkward. My job was to continue holding the space no matter what she was experiencing. When the first round of breathing was done, we began talking about her experience during it. She told me her reactions and thoughts and feelings, including what had been stirred up from her history of relationships with men from her father to the guy she was currently dating. When I began to respond it was Merlin who spoke, and I was amazed to hear someone else's words coming out of me. I remained conscious of what was happening the whole time.

Through me, he explained to her why she had created the dynamics with men in her life that she had and exactly in what ways this was an important part of her karmic education. He went into how she could make peace with this history and understand how to move forward in the present moment. The core message included that her distrust of men because of how they treated her was in truth about her distrust of herself for choosing those to be in her life who were not the right men for her to be around. The solution to that would be to listen to herself and trust her inner radar and wisdom, but to begin with forgiving herself for her choices in the past.

This conversation between them was around just under a half hour, and then we did a second round of the breathing exercise. This time she felt able to relax easily and fully into the space I created. This round was around a third the duration of the first yet many times more productive, as she felt alright with allowing herself to relax into herself.

The impact in her life was immediate. She told me she had not felt safe in the company of a man since she was about four years old until that night. A particular memory came back to her when we were breathing together, of crawling at that age into her dad's arms after he had fallen asleep sitting up on the couch. That was an important feeling for her to reconnect to, and it was a sort of barometer for how powerful her choice to relax into trusting could be. The following day she called the man she was dating to discuss a few things openly and directly, recognizing that she had to do this to honor herself. The relationship had begun without a clear intention on her part and until she spoke with him it had threatened to be a repeat of an old, unhappy pattern with men after which she would feel disrespected and without reason to respect herself.

The channel over which Merlin speaks and operates is related to personal alchemy and magic, which includes sexual energy. I could see the similarities between him, Thoth, and St. Germain, at least in taking in truths and the basic tenets of natural law in order to adjust to living within and flowing with the big picture. Yet this was different. The energy of Merlin seems to me to belong in the alchemical-sex-magical realm of tantra.

A White Light

I found myself one night reading an online biography of Martin Luther King, Jr. Photos have been one way I can tap into other people's energies, including photos of those who have passed away. Their stories can jump out at me if I let them and so I often avoid old photos of dead people unless it's focused on mediumship or research. For an unknown reason I lingered on King's photo after I read the biography and after a minute or so – which feels like a long time to look into the eyes of someone in a photo – I felt a slight pull to open to the energy coming from him. I continued to look and began to open to it and a full, rich, powerful energy began to descend in the room and surround me. I could tell that it was a source stronger than anything I had ever worked with and that the energy in the room was just a fraction of it. Being pretty freaked out from the intensity, I asked it to stop where it was. I said I would open to what it had so far brought, but that I wasn't sure I could handle any more of it right then.[23]

---

[23] Part of me wants to regret not opening more, given the effects opening a little yielded that you'll read about in a moment. Yet having strong and healthy boundaries involves knowing and being honest with yourself about what you can and cannot handle in any given moment. There's no objective judgment that can apply, and the rest of me is clear I did what was right for me at that time.

I spent time adjusting to it being in the room and letting myself feel into it. In the past I had experienced what I call software upgrades – when some corner of my consciousness got dusted off and something was plugged in so I could proceed in the direction I intended. Working with Thoth, et al. had brought some of these and others came in dreams or during meditation with my guides. This was different from those experiences and more potent than any of them. Working with different sorts of energies had taught me about the different vibrations that various beings carry, and I had never felt this vibration before. It was "whiter" or higher, more – I guess – "pure" than any I'd encountered, hence its intensity.

This vibration is that of truth, and the teaching of the being who brought it to me is that when you align fully with truth, you cannot help but think, speak, and live it. Said another way, you cannot help but live your life aligned with a truth once you take in its vibration. Martin Luther King, Jr. is a stellar example of this. His astrological birth chart viewed through the lens of karma says that his soul's mission centers on learning to be empowered through thinking and speaking from the heart and in powerful ways.[24] He could have gone about developing power

---

[24] His Pluto was in the 3rd house, the part of the chart about perception and communication, and the sign of Cancer, related to feeling and expressing emotion.

of mind and speech in many different ways. In some lives, that soul is doing all sorts of things to figure out what such power is. In the life in which we know this soul as Martin Luther King, Jr., his spiritual side and his connection to his heart contributed to his definition of power.

The power in his voice to which many have responded by getting in touch their own power was the result of his alignment with truth. Everything he undertook and spoke about was grounded in what he knew to be true – not what he *thought* might be true or what he thought *was* true, but what he felt in his entire being was true. His persona vibrated with truth and he had a tremendous impact on people around him and the world in general.

While this energy was with me, tuning me up, I began to see the difference between being committed to honesty and being aligned with truth. With the former, you choose to live an ethical life whether inspired by a desire to tell the truth or a fear of lying – which are, in fact, very different. With the latter, you cannot help but live in accordance with what you know is true. The former can have a lot to do with thoughts about what is true while the latter precludes thought and connects you to the vibration of truth. I had always valued truth and for a long time had been committed to honesty, but this energy represented another level regarding truth I had not known even existed.

I saw that this tune up was exactly what I had been asking for, as for a few years I had been vacillating between a handful of thoughts and attitudes about what is good for me based in "should": *I should eat better, I should exercise more*, etc. Such statements are the result of fear-based thinking and I knew they weren't working. Creating intentions based in fear is a guarantee that it won't come to fruition.

When I realized that I was falling asleep in my chair – it was after two in the morning – I thanked the energy and told it I needed to go to bed. It began to withdraw and I felt the room clear out, but its vibration didn't leave me. I had a profound sense of peace and clarity and I was perhaps the most peaceful and clear that I've ever been.

This experience allowed me to tap into the feeling of dishonesty that accompany choices not in integrity or based in fear. I had made a commitment to myself to live in honest ways and aligned with truth, but I needed such a tune up to be sensitive enough to be able to call myself on anything that wasn't aligned with truth. My 6th chakra or third eye felt wide open in a new way and supercharged. I was carrying that vibration in the rest of my body, too.

The next evening I went to a meeting for the teachers of a group through which I was offering classes. The discussion was to be about how to develop a liability waiver system to protect the group and its facilitators and organizer from anything that could go wrong during the healing classes offered there. I felt clear that the entire conversation was based in fear and wasn't sure how to respond. I was frustrated that they couldn't see this, and unfortunately my anger came out in my reactions to it. I was sitting in a circle of people who identify as healers, all nodding their heads practically in unison with vibration that affirmed, "Yes, the world *is* a dangerous place and yet, we *do* have to protect ourselves." It was beyond clear to me that if you believe there are reasons to be afraid, you will draw to you situations and people to give you reasons to be afraid.

Over the following few weeks I tuned up to that energy on a daily basis first thing in the morning. One major result was that I was able to decouple fully my emotions from my eating habits. I had known for years everything a person could know about this kind of situation and healing it, but I needed some final push to be able to feel into the vibration of what I was doing when I ate things my body didn't like or want. I had also learned to eat what my body *did* want, yet I was at times eating what didn't feel right to eat. I'd been living and teaching others that one's body offers you messages all the time about things happening in one's life and that there is a skill in learning to listen, and that doing so is key to health. Getting this tune up enabled me to feel instantly into what around me didn't feel true, and with food choices it came down to how I wanted to feel. Did I want to be happy and energized enough to do the work I'm passionate about doing? Was I willing to be totally honest with myself about what behaviors and patterns I chose to persist in that kept me from being able to do that?

The affirmative answer had been in place for years in my mind, and I was able to see things with clarity now and adjust my behaviors. This lead to a transition back into eating a mostly raw diet. I had several years prior eaten that way, but with occasional deviations with foods that didn't make me feel good and didn't support my goals. I had a lot of judgments about food, centered on shoulds. Being able to attune to this energy of truth is a gift I appreciate for many reasons, perhaps mostly for the opportunity to take my skills in discernment to the next, deeper, and more personal level. Having had this experience, a chapter felt complete. It also seemed time to write out many of the experiences that I had had over the previous seven years, as I'd been advised by wise friends and guides for years that I would. They reflected to me that while each person's process is unique, I was in a position to articulate some of the basic spiritual principles I had been lead through learning and that those principles were useful for many people.

The process of opening happens in stages. At present, as I finish this recounting of the last seven years, I have some ideas about what's next. But, as always, I might get some surprises and be lead in a direction I could not have expected.

It's an adventure. This process asks me to trust, and I'm getting better and better at it. If you were drawn to this book you might be being asked to figure out what you need to do in order to trust life, yourself, and the Universe a little (or a lot) more. However that might look in your life, be easy on yourself. Opening to spirit can be a difficult process and you'll need to remember to take care of yourself well. Actually, if spirit's asking you to do anything new or in better ways, it's probably that!

Appendix: A Meditation

A few times I've mentioned the importance of having a meditation practice of some kind for those wanting to open to and develop their intuitive/psychic side. This appendix offers you a meditation I learned in channeling class that I use in my life and when I work with clients. I teach it to clients and students, too, as it is so valuable for so many reasons. A number of those to whom I've taught it have worked with elements of it in other meditations and have told me that this particular combination is unique and beneficial. They feel the effects of it immediately and the benefits grow over time.

This meditation is for grounding, opening to spirit, opening the heart, feeding your aura, clearing out your energy system, and setting healthy boundaries. I offer a 13-minute MP3 version of it through my website (tdjacobs.com) if you prefer being lead in meditation by someone else.

Following it will be notes on its different sections.

The Meditation

Sit in a comfortable position with your spine straight. Close your eyes. Let your breathing be slow, relaxed, and deep. Notice where you are holding tension in your body and let it go over a few exhales. Some tension will naturally want to leave quickly, some will not. Let this be okay.

Begin sending energetic cords from your root or 1st chakra (located around the anus) and from the soles of your feet down into the Earth. Send them further down on each exhale with your target being the center of the Earth. Do this until the cords are strong, and then imagine them becoming wider while remaining strongly in place. If for some reason this is not comfortable or does not make sense, simply focus on these three points (root chakra and the bottoms of your feet) and strongly intend to open them to the energy of the Earth.

Breathe energy from the Earth up through these cords (or invite and allow it), letting it fill your whole body. Allow it to come up through your torso to your shoulders, and down your arms to the ends of your fingers. Allow it to come up to your neck and to the top of your head. Do this for a minute or two.

Next, on each exhale begin sending the energy you bring up on each inhale back down the cords to the Earth. Let the energy fill you on each inhale and send all of it back down on each exhale.

Continue for 3 minutes.

Leaving those cords intact, put your attention on your crown or 7th chakra, the top of your head. Open it and send a cord from your crown up to the center of the cosmos. On every exhale extend the cord further toward the center of the cosmos. Imagine that cord getting wider. Do this for a minute or two.

Intend that supportive, loving energy from the cosmos, the universe, or your guides come to you. Breathe this energy from the cosmos in through your this cord from your crown, letting it fill your body and get all the way down your arms to your fingers and all the way down your legs to your toes. Do this for a minute or two.

Now begin sending the energy back on the exhales, still taking it in on the inhales.

Continue for 3 minutes.

Next, open your root and your crown at the same time. Breath in from each source simultaneously, and breathe out to each source simultaneously. Feel each energy come into your body and fill you.

Continue for 3 minutes.

Continue breathing energy in from each source at the same time. Now on each exhale, send all the energy you have breathed in from the two sources out through your 4th chakra, your heart center, located in the middle of your chest. Imagine a cord of white light coming out of the center of your chest. Let it wrap around you as it will.

Periodically enlarge the opening in your heart center and the width of the cord of white light. Focus on generating energy from your heart center on every exhale. You should feel more open and expansive the more you do this.

Continue for 3 minutes.

Say silently or aloud 3 times:

All energies that cannot match my frequency of love must leave now.

Draw your aura, what surrounds you that you have been feeding with the white light, to the center of your body. Squeeze it and send the whole thing down the cord from your root chakra into the Earth. Let it go. When it is clean it will come back up on its own and take its natural shape around you.

Notes

This meditation creates a space for clarity. At the end of it is when I begin working with my guides or on a personal issue. I usually do it before working with clients because it lets me put myself into a receptive space in which I am open and clear to feel and sense into things. By doing I ensure that I'm grounded, my mind is clear, my heart is open, and I'm ready for any issue a client might bring to me in order to receive clarity, assistance, and support.

The meditation is a process of opening. *No matter how many times you do it, it is each time a process of opening.* Our energies and feelings vary over time and so if you do the meditation on a regular basis, expect to find different parts of it easier and less easy on different days depending on what's going on in your life at any given time. There might be no rhyme or reason for it or it might be telling you about what's up in your energy system that needs to be reviewed.

Whatever happens, observe the process. Some find it useful to make notes about how the process changes for them over time. Even if you choose not to use it, it can be a good idea to keep a notebook next to you in case you choose to work with your guides at the end of the meditation or ask others or your higher self for guidance.

Choose to be good to yourself. Let go of any judgments you might of yourself if some part of it is difficult for you to do or stirs up something in your field that's difficult to work with. If you do the meditation on a regular basis, you'll become practiced in creating a space of clarity for yourself that will allow you to see your life consistently through your spiritual eyes.

Grounding is the beginning of the process because we must have a firm foundation to do intuitive or psychic work well. Without it we risk becoming stereotypes of flakey psychics that no one wants to listen to! It's easy to pull ideas and what looks like or may be fact out of the ethers. Grounding helps us discern what in the ethers is useful and it helps us manage our health as we engage in intuitive or psychic work.

If you found sending cords through your root chakra down into the earth difficult or impossible, don't lose heart. It could mean that you're simply not used to such a thing. It could also mean that your root chakra is in some way blocked. If you have issues with your faith in your ability to survive or your feeling of having a tribe to belong to, you might be carrying stuck energy in your root chakra. Don't fret! Blocks in chakras are common for many people and each and every one can be dealt with. Among those I've taught this meditation, this step is often the most difficult one. I recommend Caroline Myss's *Anatomy of the Spirit* for tips and tricks to working through such issues.

Opening the crown allows us to connect with the spiritual realms. Intuitive and psychic work can be done using the talents of the 6th chakra (much to do with intuition) yet opening and flushing out the 7th chakra ensures that one can become aligned with the highest levels of truth. Then the 6th chakra is free to pick right and timely things out of the ethers because the person is aligned with truth and not simply getting information.

If you found opening this chakra and sending a cord out of it difficult, you might have some blocks in this chakra. It relates to our willingness to trust the Universe and the perfection of its unfolding plan. It is our route to connect with our spiritual nature.

Of all the people I've taught the meditation to, opening the crown is often the easiest part. Those drawn to spiritual paths often find it comfortable to seek and be connected to this energy. We are often taught that spirituality is about what is called ascension – reaching up to and developing a relationship with spirit. We can forget to include descension in our process. This is grounding into the Earth and developing healthy relationships with our bodies. It asks us to view our bodies as necessary parts of our spiritual journeys and not hindrances we have to put up with while here. Traveling the path of descension rounds out our spiritual training and is very important.

Another step many find difficult is opening the 4th chakra or heart center. We are often taught to avoid this and suspect that if we do it, we could be overly emotional or, even, emotional wrecks overflowing with embarrassing outbursts. For those of us who do not learn to manage our emotional nature in healthy ways, our heart centers might be clogged up with active, living memories of past pain, grief, shame, and/or regret. When a person knows intuitively or consciously that this is the case, he or she will be hesitant to open the heart so he or she doesn't unleash an unmanageable flood of feeling and lose control of the self.

At times during the first couple of years that I did the meditation on a regular basis (beginning with channeling class), a number of times I found myself simply unwilling to open my heart. At those times I happened to be angry or hurt about something and I wasn't willing to let go of it in that moment – I wasn't done being angry or hurt. Anger and pain can be dissolved with heart energy – it is truly healing energy – but there are times when we're not ready to stop being angry or hurt. Some of these times I persisted in trying to open my heart (sometimes for over 20 minutes on just this step, which could feel like 12 consecutive eternities when in that sort of pained and angry space), and at other times I came back to it later. It is important to learn to let go of any judging voice that might come up about how well you are doing the meditation. Sitting down to do the meditation is always better than not doing so – even if you do just part of it.

When you generate energy from your heart center, it is love that you generate. Plain and simple. Most of us react with love to circumstances and individuals in our lives. Think of your reaction to seeing loved ones including family, friends, and pets. Not many of us generate love because we choose to do so. This part of the meditation is very important for learning to manage your own energy. When you have developed a willingness to generate love no matter what's happening around you, two important things become true.

1. You maintain a positive, loving attitude toward yourself and others no matter what is happening around you.
2. You have a positive, loving effect on the world around you.

For those who have not been taught that if you want to have love in your life you must create it yourself, this meditation is a great tool. We can all benefit from overcoming the conditioning that love comes from somewhere else.

Once you have generated energy from your heart center – love – for a while, stating that what cannot match its frequency must leave is a powerful way to set a positive boundary. A negative boundary would be something like, "I want negativity to leave," but negative boundaries reinforce and increase negativity, drawing it to you. To see through our spiritual eyes we must learn to rephrase our thoughts and intentions to get in touch with the power of creativity language carries when we learn to use it in positive ways.

When you set this boundary during the meditation, energies that can match it and raise it are the ones that stay. The effect lasts longer than the meditation yet for most of us, negative thoughts and emotions will come up again later. Doing the meditation consistently over a long period of time will tip the balance out of negativity, and this is when your life can truly change for the better.

Once you've set this boundary, squeezing your aura out and sending it down the cords from your root chakra is to leave what doesn't match the loving frequency with the Earth. Some people think that sending negative energy to any other entity might be a violation or violent, but the Earth is willing to take it and knows what to do with it.

About The Author

Tom Jacobs is an Evolutionary Astrologer, Medium, and Channel. A graduate of Evolutionary Astrologer Steven Forrest's Apprenticeship Program, he has an active practice of readings and coaching to help people understand what they came to Earth to do and supporting them in making it happen. Tom is the author or channel of 15 books on astrology, mythology, and spirituality and original astrological natal reports on Chiron, Lilith, and the shifts happening now that culminated in 2012. He offers a groundbreaking audio course on Chiron based on channelings from Djehuty, "Chiron, 2012, and the Aquarian Age: The Key and How to Use It."

Contact Tom Jacobs via http://tdjacobs.com.

Made in the USA
San Bernardino, CA
08 December 2017